THE ROOF OF THE WORLD

ENCYCLOPEDIA OF
DISCOVERY AND EXPLORATION

16
THE ROOF OF
THE WORLD

BY GEOFFREY HINDLEY

Aldus Books London

Executive Coordinators: Beppie Harrison
John Mason
Design Director: Guenther Radtke
Editorial: Ann Craig
Jill Gormley
Marjorie Dickens
Picture Editor: Peter Cook
Research: Elizabeth Lake

Contents

Left: Mountaineering today is an advanced science, but it still demands the utmost skill and courage from climbers. Ian Clough, a British climber seen here on the south face of Annapurna in 1970, was killed by an ice fall on the descent.

Frontispiece: It was a Swiss scientist, Horace Bénédict de Saussure, whose passion for Mont Blanc launched the great age of mountaineering. Here he is seen leading his party down after climbing Mont Blanc in 1787.

List of Maps

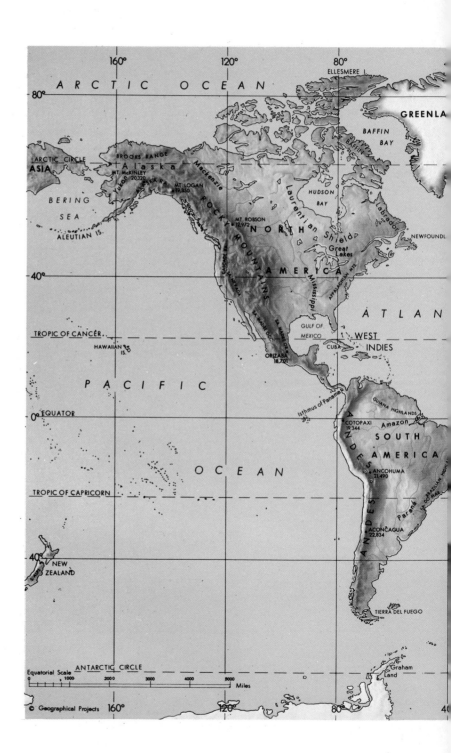

This relief map picks out in shades of brown the principal mountain ranges of the world. Many of the world's highest peaks are shown, together with their heights in feet above sea level.

ARCTIC OCEAN

SPITZBERGEN

NOVAYA
ZEMLYA

NEW SIBERIAN IS.

ARCTIC CIRCLE

ICELAND

Taimyr Pena.

Siberian
Plateau

VERKHOYANSK RA.

Lena

KOLYMA RA.

Kamchatka

BERING SEA

GLITTERTIND
8100

Scandinavia

Siberian
Ob
Plain

Yenisei

Lena

Stanovoi
Plat.

BRITISH
ISLES

E   U   R   O   P   E

URALS

A   S   I   A

Amur

SAKHALIN

ALEUTIAN IS.

MT. BLANC
15,781

CARPATHIANS

Volga

CASPIAN SEA

ARAL
SEA

POBEDY PEAK
24,406

ALTAY

Gobi

40°

ELBRUS
18,481

CAUCASUS

COMMUNISM PEAK
24,590

TIEN SHAN

NAN SHAN

Danube

BLACK SEA

ELBURZ

ZAGROS MTS.

PAMIRS

HINDUKUSH

MT. GODWIN AUSTEN
(K2) 28,250

KARAKORAM RA.

Plateau
of
Tibet

MT. FUJI 12,388

JAPAN

PACIFIC

MEDITERRANEAN SEA

Indus

HIMALAYA

Yangtze R.

MINYA KONKA
24,900

GT. ATLAS

AHAGGAR
MTS.

TIBESTI
MASSIF

Nile

Arabian

Peninsula

ARABIAN
SEA

MT. EVEREST
29,028

Deccan

Ganges

Mekong

TROPIC OF CANCER

HAWAIIAN
IS.

Sahara

A F R I C A

Niger

BAY OF
BENGAL

PHILIPPINE
IS.

MT. CAMEROON
13,350

CEYLON

SUMATRA

BORNEO

SOUTH CHINA SEA

O   C   E   A   N

RUWENZORI RA.

MT. KENYA
17,058

NEW
GUINEA

EQUATOR

L. Victoria

KILIMANJARO
19,340

I   N   D   I   A   N

Congo

Zambezi

MAROMOKOTRO
9450

MADAGASCAR

CORAL SEA

CEAN

MT. AUX
SOURCES
10,822

DRAKENSBERG

O   C   E   A   N

AUSTRALIA

GT. DIVIDING RA.

TROPIC OF CAPRICORN

MT. KOSCIUSKO
7316

T A S M A N

40°

TASMANIA

SEA

MT. COOK
12,349

NEW
ZEALAND

S   O   U   T   H   E   R   N   O   C   E   A   N

ANTARCTIC CIRCLE

A   N   T   A   R   C   T   I   C   A

Why Do Men Climb Mountains?

1

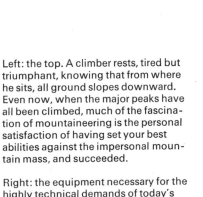

A man clings to a precarious hold high on the sheer face of a mountain. Slowly, straining every nerve and muscle, he inches his way upward. One slip, and he could plummet thousands of feet down to the rocks below. But despite the danger, he takes intense pleasure in this struggle to reach the soaring summit above him. Why? What is it that makes men risk their lives to climb mountains?

The question is difficult to answer simply, although many reasons for climbing can be found. One of these, of course, is the desire for conquest. The will to meet and master a significant adversary is as old as man himself. Just as basic is the instinct to explore the unknown—to place one's feet on a lofty portion of the earth never trod before, or to pioneer a new route to a summit already reached.

Love of adventure is another vital part of the climber's motivation. Unforeseen hazards and swiftly changing conditions make every ascent a unique and exciting experience, stretching a man's capacities to the full and giving his life a heightened intensity. Although the

Left: the top. A climber rests, tired but triumphant, knowing that from where he sits, all ground slopes downward. Even now, when the major peaks have all been climbed, much of the fascination of mountaineering is the personal satisfaction of having set your best abilities against the impersonal mountain mass, and succeeded.

Right: the equipment necessary for the highly technical demands of today's mountain climbing hangs around the necks of two climbers on the North Face of the Eiger, ready for immediate use.

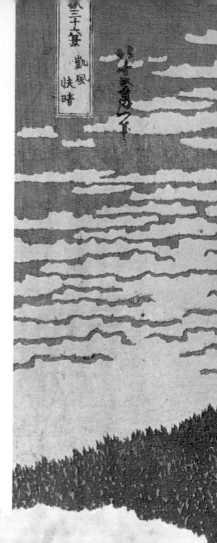

Above: in many of the world's religions, mountains have for centuries been regarded as sacred meeting places for God and man. This painting of the 1300's shows Moses receiving the Ten Commandments on Mount Sinai.

mountaineer does n̶̶̶ ̶̶̶ ̶̶̶ ̶̶̶ ̶̶̶ own sake, he willingly ac̶ ̶̶̶ ̶̶̶ ̶̶̶ ̶t climbing and, in a sense, even welcc̶ ̶̶̶ ̶̶̶ ̶of his ingenuity, endurance, skill, and courage. And ̶ ̶̶̶ ̶g of adventure that draws the members of a team together, orging the strong bond of comradeship that mountaineers so often speak of as one of the great rewards of climbing.

For some men, a successful climb is a matter of personal pride and prestige, quite frankly, something to boast about. For others, it may be that confronting the elemental dangers of the mountains is a way of finding relief and refreshment from the exhausting complexities of everyday life. Indeed, the "call of the wild" plays a large part in the mind and heart of every climber. High above the polluted air and congested streets of the world's cities, he can renew his essential kinship with the natural world. On a deeper level, some mountaineers experience an almost mystical sense of communion with nature amidst the rugged beauty and breathtaking views of the mountains. The Australian climber Herbert Tichy once spoke of this in describing the last few minutes of a Himalayan ascent. "The world

around me showed a kindly ~~~~~~~ I had never before experienced," he wrote. "S~~~~~~~~~~~ and myself were an indivisible and divine whole~~~~~~~~~~~

Mountains have been climbed~~~~~~~ diverse as the pursuit of scientific research and the winning of a wager. And, in the fierce international rivalry of modern times, they have even been climbed in the interests of national prestige. These, like all the other "reasons" for climbing, have been sufficient to spur men on to the highest achievement. Yet none of them alone fully explains the powerful attraction of mountaineering.

Perhaps, as the famed Himalayan climber George Leigh Mallory once remarked, men climb mountains simply, "Because they are there." For the true mountaineer, there is at the heart of it all an obsession that cannot, and need not, be explained. Whatever it may be that starts him climbing, there comes a time when the mountains themselves become his only reason. They take on a personality, and he becomes a part of their world. When this happens, there is no objective worthy of the name but the climb itself, and in that climb, the mountaineer finds fulfillment.

This being so, another question raises itself: Why have men not always climbed mountains? For until the 1800's, mountaineering as such hardly existed. History records but a scant number of ascents before that time, and even these were mostly undertaken for purely practical reasons. To climb a mountain for pleasure was virtually unheard of, and the rare men who did so risked being thought highly eccentric, if not mad.

From earliest times, mountains were regarded as places of mystery and terror, the source of such frightening and inexplicable phenomena as glaciers, avalanches, and volcanic eruptions. For this reason, early man soon came to believe that mountain summits were the dwelling places of the gods. Peaks such as Mount Olympus and Mount Parnassus in Greece, Popocatépetl in Mexico, Everest on the Tibet-Nepal border, and Mount Fuji in Japan, became the object of reverence. But only in the East were mountains revered for their own sake. In ancient India, China, and Japan, for example, mountains often served as a source of inspiration for poets, artists, and philosophers. But in the Western world, and particularly in ancient

Above: one of the most remarkable feats of maneuver in the mountains was accomplished in 218 B.C. when Hannibal, the Carthaginian general, led his army across the Alps to attack the Roman army unexpectedly at the rear.

Right: for years men avoided mountains. But in 1336 an Italian poet named Francesco Petrarch, inspired by the paintings of Leonardo da Vinci and spurred on by a stubborn desire to reach the top, climbed Mont Ventoux.

Greece and Rome, men saw nothing beautiful or inspiring about mountains. Far from giving them pleasure or exciting their curiosity, the snowy peaks on their horizons filled them with dread and aversion, and they did their best to ignore all but the handful of peaks to which they had attached religious significance.

Only a few real climbs are known to have been made during classical times. Two of these—the ascent of a Balkan peak by Philip of Macedonia in 350 B.C., and the ascent of Mount Etna by the Emperor Hadrian in the A.D. 100's—were undertaken simply to gratify royal whims. Philip wanted to discover whether both the Adriatic and the Aegean seas could be viewed from a single vantage point, and Hadrian wished to see the sunrise from a mountaintop. A far more heroic undertaking occurred in the winter of 218 B.C., when the Carthaginian general Hannibal led his army across the Alps to launch a surprise attack on the Romans from the north.

But in ancient times, the only known case of a climb made for reasons of curiosity and pleasure was the ascent of Mount Etna, in the 400's B.C., by the philosopher Empedocles. And it was to be many centuries before another such climb was made, for the traditional dislike and disinterest in mountains continued to prevail in the West long after the fall of Rome and the rise of Christendom. In fact, during the early Middle Ages, men became, if possible, even less interested in mountains.

The emphasis placed by Christianity on the relationship between God and man resulted, to a degree, in the devaluing of nature. Mountains, together with all the physical world, were viewed as being less real than the world of spiritual concerns, and were therefore thought unworthy of serious notice. This attitude was reflected not only in medieval paintings, which rarely included landscapes, but also in medieval maps, which frequently omitted to show the locations of even the loftiest peaks in the areas they depicted.

The start of the Renaissance heralded the reawakening of men's interest in the natural world. Scholars began to take a scientific approach to natural phenomena. Artists—chief among them Leonardo da Vinci—began to depict natural scenes with superb accuracy and appreciation. It is perhaps not so surprising, then, that the first known ascent of an Alpine peak should have occurred during this period. The climber was the poet Petrarch, who, on April 26, 1336, ascended Mont Ventoux (6,263 feet) in southern France. From a letter he wrote to his father describing the ascent, it is clear that he made the climb for no other reason than to reach the top, and that he relished both the climb and the glorious view he saw from the summit.

But Petrarch's historic ascent was not emulated by others, and nearly two centuries elapsed before the joys of climbing were discovered by another man, the Swiss scientist Konrad Von Gesner. Perhaps it was in search of botanical specimens that Gesner first began climbing in the mid-1500's. But whatever the reason, he soon became an ardent mountaineer. He made it a rule to climb one

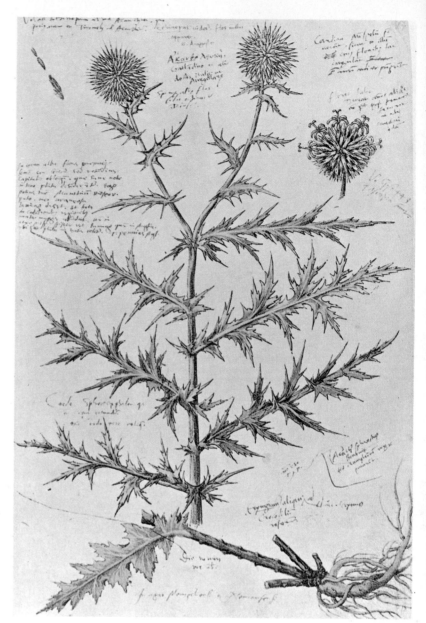

Above: another early mountaineer was Konrad Von Gesner, a Swiss scientist who began to climb the mountains of the Alps to find botanical specimens for his collection. This painting, by Tobias Stimmer, shows Gesner in 1564.

Above right: a thistle *(Echinops Sphaerocephalus)* drawn by Gesner. Having begun climbing to collect plants, Gesner became so interested in the enjoyment of climbing itself that he made it a rule to scale a peak a year.

mountain every year "at the time when the flowers are at their best," and wrote movingly of the rapture that overwhelmed him in the awesome silence of the heights.

In the meantime, at the bidding of Charles VIII of France, the first ascent of the 6,880-foot Alpine peak Mont Aiguille had been made. This climb, led by the king's chamberlain, De Beaupré, in 1492, was an impressive achievement, planned and carried out with much skill. Nonetheless, it was a matter of pure duty. Having done his sovereign's command, De Beaupré never climbed another mountain.

During the next two centuries, an increasing number of European traders and travelers journeyed through the Alps, toiling over the major passes on foot and on horseback. None of these journeys was undertaken for pleasure, but they did contribute substantially to what was then known about Alpine terrain and weather conditions. As early as 1574, a book called *Concerning the Difficulties of Alpine Travel* was written by one Josias Simler of Zurich. In it he offered travelers much useful advice about the avoidance of avalanches and hidden crevasses, and about the use of ropes and crampons as climbing aids.

People listened to the Alpine travelers' tales of blizzards, glaciers, crevasses, and dizzying views with mixed horror and curiosity. By the early 1700's, in search of the picturesque and the "finely horrid," a few people had begun venturing into the mountains. Two such tourists were the Englishmen William Windham and Richard Pococke. These men set forth in 1741 to explore the glaciers in the region of Chamonix, a French mountain village very near the point where the borders of France, Italy, and Switzerland meet. As an "expedition," the venture hardly merits the name, for, despite elaborate preparations, the party went only as far as the Montenvers Pass, to which a path already existed. However, their trip set a fashion for walking in the Alps.

One man who did more than walk in the Alps was Father Placidus á Spescha, a Benedictine monk, who, in the later 1700's, made a series of astonishing climbs there. Many of the peaks he scaled were over 10,000 feet, and all of them he climbed for the sheer joy of it. But although many people today consider him to be the real father of mountaineering, his daring ascents created little stir at the time. Indeed, people's curiosity about mountains might have gone no farther than Alpine "rambles" had it not been for the scientists of the period.

European scholars had first become curious about mountains in the late 1600's. The tales of Alpine travelers intrigued them and they were eager to investigate the phenomena described to them. But beyond this, they sought to understand the very existence of mountains which baffled them by their utter uselessness. Little was known about geology, and scientists were at a loss to explain the whys and wherefores of geographic features.

Today we know that the geography of the earth is the result of continual change and movement over millions of years of geologic time. The world's mountain ranges are the product of these changes. There are four basic types of mountains. *Volcanic mountains* form

Above: one of the earliest Englishmen to be fascinated by the Alpine region was Richard Pococke, seen here in Oriental costume, who set out with a friend, William Windham, to explore the glaciers around Chamonix in 1741.

Below: one of the most frightening
hazards for men in the mountains has
always been the avalanche, when a
wall of snow and rock collapses
suddenly and crashes downward, bury-
ing everything that lies in its path. This
drawing of 1849 shows an avalanche
sweeping down a mountainside.

Above: a marine fossil, 130 million years old. It was discovered 18,000 feet up in the Himalaya, showing that this range was once beneath the sea.

when lava and ashes burst through the earth's crust. Some still display the cones of extinct or living volcanoes. *Dome mountains* form when the top section of the earth's crust rises into domes like huge blisters. *Faultblock mountains* form when the earth's crust breaks into great blocks, some of which move upward, while some move downward. *Folded mountains* form when the earth's crust wrinkles into wavelike forms. One of the theories put forward to explain this last phenomenon is that, as the earth's center cools, its surface contracts, causing a wrinkling in the strata beneath the earth's crust. But whatever the cause, the forces are huge and have pushed up mountain peaks of tremendous heights. In the Himalaya, fossil forms of marine life can be found at 18,000 feet—indicating that in some remote past this mountain range was once the floor of a sea.

Once the rock stratum has been thrust above the earth's surface, it becomes subject to weathering. As the softer strata are worn away by the action of massive, slow-moving glaciers, deep valleys are gouged out, leaving jagged peaks. Then these angularities, too, are worn down by wind and rain until, after thousands and thousands

Once the rock layer, the basic material of the mountain, has been thrust up, erosion begins wearing it away. One form of erosion is by massive rivers of slow-moving ice, which carve out deep valleys. The glacier shown in this engraving is the Rheinwald, which is one source of the Rhine River.

of years, a once formidable mountain range has become a series of gently undulating hills. Today, geologists believe that the Russian Urals and the American Appalachians—without mountains in the climber's sense of the word—began to form some 300 million years ago. The formation of the Alps, on the other hand, seems to have begun about 30 million years ago, with the uplift reaching its climax about 1 million years ago. The Himalaya are also quite young and, as a system, may be said to be still developing.

All this was not known in the mid-1700's, when the science of geology was still in its infancy. But a few European thinkers were

beginning to realize—a century before Charles Darwin formulated his theory of evolution—that the history of the earth stretched back many thousands of years and that the world was far older than the Bible's accounts suggested.

One such man, the Swiss scientist Horace Bénédict de Saussure, looked to the mountains for evidence to support his theories. But once in the Alps, his scientific interest in all mountains swiftly changed to a passion for one mountain in particular—Mont Blanc. And it was to be De Saussure's passion for this mountain that launched the great age of mountaineering.

19

The Beginnings 2

Horace Bénédict de Saussure, the scientist who opened men's eyes to the joys of mountaineering, was born in Geneva in 1740. Very early in his life he showed an extraordinary gift for observation and deduction, and, by the age of 20, was already establishing his reputation as a scientist. In 1760, he went to the Alpine tourist resort of Chamonix to make a study of glaciers. There it was that he first saw Mont Blanc. Towering to a height of 15,781 feet, the mountain's snowy, dome-like summit seemed to beckon to him.

De Saussure's first thought was to establish a scientific research center high on the mountainside, but he could find no one who

would assist him in the project. In fact, his proposed plan to climb the mountain provoked widespread horror and disbelief. Many of the peasants of the region had clambered over the lower slopes and glaciers of Mont Blanc while hunting chamois (a kind of mountain goat), but none had ever dared venture higher than a few thousand feet. They believed that demons and dragons guarded the heights, and despite the young scientist's pleas, they could not be induced to take part in an expedition to the summit.

But De Saussure only became more determined to climb Mont Blanc. Its beauty, as he put it later, had begun to disturb his feelings

Horace Bénédict de Saussure, a Swiss scientist, fulfilled his ambition in 1787 by reaching the summit of Mont Blanc. He was accompanied by 18 guides and supplies, including a basket of bottled wine to celebrate the climb.

21

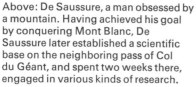

Above: De Saussure, a man obsessed by a mountain. Having achieved his goal by conquering Mont Blanc, De Saussure later established a scientific base on the neighboring pass of Col du Géant, and spent two weeks there, engaged in various kinds of research.

like some kind of illness. "I could not even look upon the mountain, which is visible from so many points round about, without being seized with an aching of desire," he wrote later. For a scientist, particularly during the Age of Reason, this was a most unobjective approach, and De Saussure himself could never fully explain the passion that Mont Blanc had inspired in him. In fact, he was at heart a true mountaineer, long before the word itself came into use. Nevertheless, he always found it hard to admit that something more than scientific curiosity lay behind his repeated journeys to the mountains. In the course of these journeys, he did, however, carry on much important research, and his great work, *Voyages in the Alps*,

is recognized as a landmark in the developing science of geology. It was he, for example, who first offered a rational explanation for the movement of glaciers, ascribing it simply to the pull of gravity rather than to any mysterious or magical forces.

While De Saussure was carrying out his Alpine studies, he never ceased to hope that one day he would be able to climb Mont Blanc. He even offered a reward to the first man who would pioneer a route to the summit. Fifteen years went by, and a few attempts were made in the hope of winning the reward, but all were defeated. Nor was it hard to see why. Almost nothing was known at this time about mountain terrain or climbing techniques, and above the familiar lower slopes of Mont Blanc there loomed a world of strange and frightening phenomena. It was a veritable obstacle-course of ice-walls, narrow ledges, and immense, jagged glaciers. The surface of these frozen rivers of ice was split in many places by deep fissures called crevasses. Some of these were masked by a covering of snow; others were spanned by slender ice bridges. Eerie groans could be heard coming out of the depths of these abysses from time to time. And these strange rumblings were occasionally answered by the roar of a mighty avalanche higher up, as tons of ice and snow sheered off the mountainside and crashed down the face of a cliff.

Yet despite the terrors it held, Mont Blanc appeared both incredibly lovely *and* climbable to at least one other man besides De Saussure. This man was a young Chamonix doctor named Michel Gabriel Paccard. He, too, loved the mountain and felt a compulsion to climb it. He made a series of unsuccessful attempts on the summit, but remained determined to master it—for France, for science (he always took his instruments with him), and for his own personal satisfaction.

On August 7, 1786, Paccard set off to make yet another assault on "our" mountain, as he called Mont Blanc. To help him carry his instruments, he took with him a hardy chamois-hunter named Jacques Balmat. Unlike Paccard, Balmat undertook the climb solely in the hopes of winning fame and the reward offered by De Saussure. Nonetheless, he was a strong and fearless man, already well-known for his skill in climbing Mont Blanc's lower slopes.

The two men began their climb early in the afternoon, and by late

Above: Mont Blanc, the mountain which so fascinated De Saussure, and which has beckoned to many other Alpine climbers.

Right: the shoes especially designed by De Saussure for his ascent of Mont Blanc. The soles are studded for more grip when climbing on ice and snow.

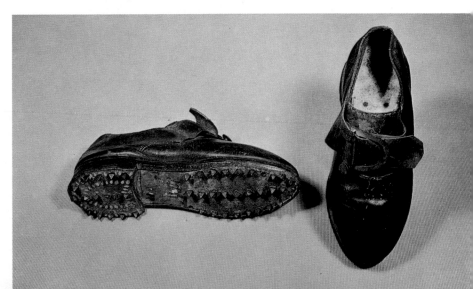

Above right: Michel Gabriel Paccard, the young Chamonix doctor who led the first successful assault on Mont Blanc. He and his guide completed the ascent with only the crudest of equipment.

Above: Jacques Balmat, the guide who accompanied Paccard on his summit climb. He later tried to claim all the credit for the historic climb himself.

evening had reached the top of a long ridge of rock called the Montagne de la Côte, where they camped for the night. In the light of early dawn they started off again, and crossed the Jonction, an ice field scored by countless crevasses. The only way they could get across several of the fissures was to lay their two alpenstocks (pointed staves) over it and crawl across them—over empty black space—to the other side. Beyond the Jonction lay a ridge of rocks called the Grands Mulets, and beyond that, two long valleys covered in deep and powdery snow. Sinking up to their hips at every step, they struggled across these valleys (now known as the Petit Plateau and the Grand Plateau) and at 3:30 P.M., reached the last major obstacle between them and the summit. This was a steep incline of ice from which arose two parallel bands of rock, the Rochers Rouges.

By now both men were frostbitten and exhausted. Moreover, they were gasping for breath in the thin air of the heights. But they pressed on, making their way between the two shoulders of rock to the gentle slopes just below the summit.

It was 6:30 P.M., when the two men stood at last, breathless but triumphant, on Mont Blanc's highest point. Tired as he was, Paccard spent an hour taking scientific measurements, and then the two started down. There was a full moon, and they managed to keep going until the early hours of the morning, when they rested again in the Montagne de la Côte, before pushing on to Chamonix. Here, Balmat duly received the reward promised by De Saussure.

For Paccard, however, the success of the climb was reward enough.

Paccard and Balmat's ascent of Mont Blanc is one of the most remarkable in mountaineering history. Not only was it the first ascent of the highest mountain in the Alps; it was achieved by a team of only two men, climbing without the benefit of even the most basic equipment—ropes, crampons (metal spikes on the underside of the boot), or ice-axes. But their triumph was to have a strange sequel. Balmat, not content with his monetary reward, began claiming that all the credit for the climb belonged to him. He boasted that he had led the entire ascent and that Paccard would never have reached the top without his help. In fact, he maintained, he had practically had to carry the doctor up the final slopes to the summit. Balmat was known to be a braggart, and his story would probably never have been believed if a journalist named Marc Bourrit, had not stepped forward to support it. Bourrit—who had tried and failed to climb Mont Blanc himself—was jealous of Paccard's success and only too pleased to spoil the doctor's triumph. He claimed that he had watched the climb through a telescope and seen Balmat take the lead.

Thus, Balmat's version of the climb came to be generally accepted, and it was not until a century later that the record was put straight with the finding of the papers of a certain Baron von Gensdorff. He had also watched the ascent through a telescope, and his notes and sketches of it prove the falsity of Balmat's claims.

For all the controversy surrounding it, and despite the fact that it was the first ascent, Paccard and Balmat's achievement on Mont Blanc was overshadowed by De Saussure's own ascent the following year. The doughty scientist had never given up his dream of climbing the mountain. He had failed on his only previous attempt, but now, after Paccard and Balmat's success, he became more than ever determined to realize his life's ambition. On August 1, 1787, he set out for the summit accompanied by no fewer than 18 guides (including his own valet, who had never even been on a mountain before!). The size of the expedition is partly explained by the number of pieces of scientific equipment that had to be carried up. When, on the afternoon of the second day, the party reached the top, De Saussure spent more than four hours conducting experiments. His only regret was that the difficulty of breathing in the rarified air of the summit forced the party to go back down before he had completed all the work he had planned. Later in the year, he

Marc Bourrit, a journalist who was frustrated many times in his efforts to climb Mont Blanc. He reacted emotionally when he learned of Paccard's successful ascent, and did his best to discredit the climb.

Left: De Saussure, with his son, coming down from the scientific base on the Col du Géant. They became so absorbed with their research that eventually the porters mutinied, and destroyed the food, forcing them down.
Below: the Alps are Europe's largest mountain system. They stretch through southeastern France, northern Italy, Switzerland, part of southern Germany, Austria, and Yugoslavia. It was in the Alps that mountaineering as we understand it really began.

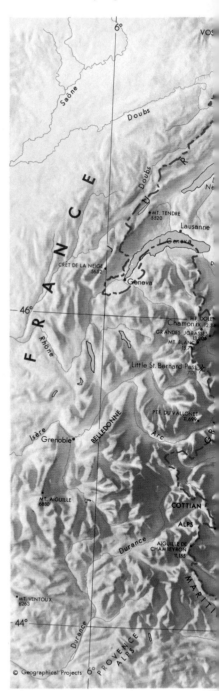

led another large expedition to a height of 10,960 feet on the Alpine pass called the Col du Géant. Once there he and his son, working in shifts, carried out a grueling series of experiments for over two weeks.

Because De Saussure was a distinguished scientist, known throughout Europe, his ascent of Mont Blanc was widely publicized. Reading the accounts of the climb, men in many different countries became fired with the ambition to emulate his achievement. Scientists and adventurers alike began to tackle Alpine peaks, and the next few decades witnessed many first ascents in the mountain chain that arches from southeastern France, through northern Italy, Switzerland, southern Germany, Austria, and into Yugoslavia.

The Alps are really composed of a number of ranges. Mont Blanc, which was climbed with increasing frequency after De Saussure's ascent, lies in the Pennine Alps to the west of the Great Saint Bernard Pass, where the frontiers of Italy, France, and Switzerland converge. From Mont Blanc the mighty Pennine Alps stretch eastward. They include such peaks as the Matterhorn (14,685 feet), the Weisshorn (14,803 feet), and the Monte Rosa (15,200 feet). To the north of the Pennines, is the loftiest of the Alpine ranges, the

Bernese Alps, where the Swiss town of Grindelwald lies surrounded by a number of mighty peaks. One of these, the famous Jungfrau (13,668 feet), was first climbed in 1811 by a wealthy Swiss merchant named Johann Meyer who, with his two sons, had explored many of the glaciers above Grindelwald. Near the Jungfrau stands the Finsteraarhorn (14,026 feet). The loftiest mountain in the Bernese Alps, it was first scaled by two Swiss guides in 1829. Two other towering peaks in the region are the Rosenhorn (12,110 feet), climbed by the German scientist Edouard Desor in 1844, and the

Left: during the early 1800's, most climbing was for scientific reasons. J. D. Forbes, a Scotsman shown here measuring a glacier, was typical of scientist-mountaineers of the period.

J. Hébert.
1838.

Right: the first woman to attempt Mont Blanc was a French countess, Henriette d'Angeville, shown here inspecting her company of guides and porters before setting out. Her stamina was remarkable, and she completed the climb.

Mittelhorn (12,166 feet), first scaled by a Scotsman, Stanhope Templeman Speer in 1845.

The thrill of climbing appealed to women as well as to men. In fact, one of the most daring climbers of this early period of mountaineering was a French countess named Henriette d'Angeville, who climbed Mont Blanc in 1838. She was followed by many other redoubtable women climbers as the century progressed. And perhaps they deserve special credit for their efforts, for not only were they venturing into what was considered a man's realm, but they had to do so in skirts. One woman, Mrs. Aubrey le Blond, who wore trousers under a detachable skirt, was forced to make two ascents of the same peak in one day, when she forgot and left her skirt on the summit. Had she not gone back to retrieve it, she would not have been permitted to enter any of the respectable inns in the valley.

Two of the most important figures in mountaineering at this time were the Scottish scientist James David Forbes and the Swiss naturalist Jean Louis Agassiz. Like De Saussure, both men justified their regular and extensive mountain expeditions on the grounds of

scientific research. But again like De Saussure, both Forbes and Agassiz reveal in their writings a passionate love for the mountains themselves.

Together, Forbes and Agassiz conducted an extensive exploration of the Unteraar Glacier in Switzerland, and, as a result of their findings, published seminal studies on the movement of glaciers. Forbes later climbed the Jungfrau, as well as other peaks in places as widely separated as Scotland, Spain, and Norway. On each of his expeditions, he took numerous scientific instruments—barometers, thermometers, polariscopes, hygrometers, hypsometers, and chronometers—and over the years added a great deal to knowledge of mountain terrain and conditions. Certainly his work was of inestimable value to science. But it was his enthusiasm for climbing that, in the end, had the greater influence on the men of his time. His writings and lectures, as well as his example, did much to encourage the growing British interest in mountaineering.

The late 1700's and early 1800's had seen the development of a literary and aesthetic movement known as Romanticism. Through the works of writers such as Goethe and Rousseau, Wordsworth,

Byron, and Shelley, nature—and mountains in particular—had come to be seen in terms of romantic peril and idyllic beauty. Even after the Romantic movement began to decline, the Romantic attitude toward mountains persisted, and even gained in intensity. The great Victorian art critic John Ruskin, for example, both painted and wrote about the beauties of the Alps with passionate awe.

British interest in mountaineering had been stirred both by the scientific exploits of James Forbes and by the lyrical writings of the Romantics. In mid-century, two events occurred to galvanize this growing interest and launch a historic period of mountaineering.

The first of these events was the well-publicized ascent of Mont Blanc in 1851 by the Englishman Albert Smith. Smith had been consumed with a desire to scale the peak since the moment in his boyhood when he had read a little book called *The Peasants of Chamonix*. He first saw the mountain when, as a student in Paris, he tramped to Chamonix in the hope of joining an expedition as a porter. He had no luck and, as he could not afford to mount an expedition of his own, he had to abandon the project. But he hung on to his dream, and in 1851, after several years of traveling and giving lectures on his experiences, he was back in Chamonix. This time, he joined up with a party of wealthy young Englishmen. They were merely touring, but when they heard that he wanted to scale Mont Blanc, they became determined to do so as well, and offered to pay for the expedition.

Although Mont Blanc had seen almost 40 ascents so far, there were still hazards enough to make the venture exciting. In 1820, three men had been killed in an avalanche on the slopes of the mountain. And even though Smith's party waited for a fine day to begin their adventure, there was still a good deal of danger in their undertaking. The route they took was in fact a very difficult one, and they were ignorant of the importance of roping up. But the weather remained fair and they were spared any serious hardships by their 36 guides and porters, who lifted them over the worst stretches. In fact, the climb went very smoothly and they returned to Chamonix much pleased with themselves.

Albert Smith did not intend to keep his triumph to himself. The very next year, at a large exhibition hall in Piccadilly, London, Smith staged a lecture-cum-picture show called "The Ascent of Mont Blanc." Londoners flocked to see and hear Smith's story, which he recounted as a huge illustrated screen was unrolled, depicting all the incidents and hazards of the adventure. Although many people later accused Smith of "vulgar showmanship," he had seized the public imagination and given an enormous boost to British interest in mountaineering.

The Bernese Alps by Josef Koch. As the mystery of mountains was slowly dispelled by growing numbers of men climbing and living on heights, the writings of early travelers inspired artists to portray their magnificence.

Above: a watercolor by the English art critic and painter John Ruskin, who felt a special reverence for mountains, although he apparently never considered climbing himself.

In 1854, another event—Sir Alfred Wills' ascent of the Wetterhorn—had an even greater impact in Britain than Smith's Mont Blanc epic. Until then, mountain climbing had been seen in terms of science, romance, and adventure. Wills' description of the Wetterhorn ascent raised mountaineering to the status of a heroic endeavor, one that called forth the best in a man and even brought him closer to God.

The Wetterhorn (12,149 feet) is not an impressively difficult climb, but Wills' description of his experience on reaching the summit was both dramatic and inspiring:

"As I took the last step . . . my left shoulder grazed against the angle of an icy embrasure, while on the right, the glacier fell abruptly away beneath me toward an unknown and awful abyss . . . I stepped across, and had passed the ridge of the Wetterhorn!

"I am not ashamed to own that I experienced, as this sublime and wonderful prospect burst upon my view, a profound and almost irrepressible emotion. We felt as in the more immediate presence of Him who had reared this tremendous pinnacle . . . poised, as it seemed, halfway between the earth and sky."

These passages from Wills' book *Wandering Among the High Alps*

Right: Albert Smith, shown here in his climbing oufit, was an Englishman who made a highly-publicized ascent of the formidable Mont Blanc in 1851.

deeply stirred many young men in Victorian England. Here, they felt, was an activity worthy of the highest sacrifice. It was fraught with hardship and peril; it demanded the utmost self-discipline and courage; and it promised a kind of exhilaration and profound satisfaction that no other sport or recreation could do.

Alfred Wills' book came out at a time when mountaineering had already gained many adherents. Nonetheless, it was to prove a landmark in the history of alpinism. For it was with this ascent of the Wetterhorn in 1854 that the so-called Golden Age of mountaineering began.

Below: Smith later presented ''dioramas,'' regaling the British public with his success. This illustrated fan served as a program.

Right: the Alpine cottage, the Eagle's Nest, used by the Wills family, some of the most enthusiastic of Victorian mountaineers during the Golden Age. Below: the Wills family at the Eagle's Nest, with Alfred Wills (holding the ice-ax at the extreme left), whose ascent of the Wetterhorn in 1854 began the era when climbing became generally accepted as a sport requiring great courage. The small boy on his mother's lap is E. F. Norton, who was leader of the 1924 attempt on Mount Everest.

The Golden Age

3

The Golden Age that began with Alfred Wills' ascent of the Wetterhorn lasted only a decade—from 1854 to 1865—but it was a decade of extraordinary mountaineering achievement. When it began, the majority of glittering peaks in Europe's mountain arc had never seen the foot of man. By its close, there was hardly a major Alpine summit that had not been climbed at least once. There was nothing planned or coordinated about this all-out assault on the Alps. Public interest and individual enthusiasm simply combined, and a new and thrilling sport was born.

The overwhelming majority of Alpine climbers during the Golden Age were British. Individually, they scored a remarkable number of historic first ascents. As a group they became known for their courage, their determination, and their passionate commitment to the sport itself. In fact, for many British climbers of the period (and for many climbers of all nationalities since then), mountaineering quickly ceased to be a sport and became a way of life. Such men returned to the Alps season after season to pit their skills against ever more difficult peaks. In so doing, they contributed to the growing body of codes and traditions, lore, and jargon that soon became an integral part of mountaineering.

The year 1857 saw a historic development in the formation of the world's first mountaineering association: the Alpine Club. Not surprisingly, the club was set up in London by a group of British climbers. Modestly begun as an association of like-minded enthusiasts, it soon acquired the status of an important society and became the leading body on all Alpine matters. It kept records, tested new equipment, and provided information about Alpine routes and conditions. In addition, it published a regular journal recording the mountaineering experiences of its members. For five years it was the only association of its kind. Then, in 1862, an Austrian counterpart was set up, followed by the formation of a Swiss Alpine Club in 1863. (Since then, hundreds of mountaineering associations have been formed all over the world.)

By and large, the members of these clubs made no pretense of climbing for any other reason than because they enjoyed it. But at least one Victorian mountaineer carried the tradition of the scientific alpinist into the new age. He was Francis Fox Tuckett, a Quaker businessman and amateur scientist who, as a young man, had met the great scientist-mountaineer James Forbes and been inspired by his

Mountaineering quickly became popular. This group of British climbers with their guides shows (back row, left to right) Melchior Anderegg, Macdonald, Grove, Jacob Anderegg, and Young Taugwalder. In the front row, left to right, Leslie Stephen, Short, Buxton, Living, and Francis Fox Tuckett. Stephen and Fox Tuckett were among the British climbers who formed the Alpine Club in London in 1857.

ideals. Between 1856 and 1874, Tuckett climbed more than 160 Alpine peaks and 370 passes. Always he took with him a vast array of scientific instruments, some being of his own invention. Festooned with apparatus, Tuckett cut a strange figure among the new generation of sportsmen climbers. Yet he stuck firmly to his belief that he, and all the other mountaineers of his generation were first and foremost pioneers exploring unknown territory. As such, he said, they were duty-bound to record, measure, and scrutinize everything they might find.

Tuckett was not entirely alone in holding this view. One of the most distinguished climbers of this period, the British physicist John Tyndall, stoutly upheld the value of science in connection with mountaineering. In fact, Tyndall's interest in climbing really came about as a result of his study of glaciers. But once in the mountains, he, like many another man before him, became an ardent alpinist. He made the first ascent of the Weisshorn (14,803 feet) in 1861 and on another occasion climbed the Monte Rosa (15,200 feet) alone, with only a flask of tea and a ham sandwich to keep him going. But even in the midst of these exploits, he never lost sight of his "real" goal—the pursuit of scientific research. And as a result of his careful observations, he made many important contributions to the developing theory of glaciers.

But men like Tuckett and Tyndall were exceptions to the rule. Most of the English mountaineers of the period climbed solely for the pleasure and satisfaction it gave them. Amateur sportsmen in the purest sense, many of them had distinguished careers in fields quite divorced from either sport or natural science. One such man was Sir Leslie Stephen, a philosopher and a leading figure in British literary life, who was also a passionate devotee of mountaineering. In 1871, Stephen turned his pen to his beloved sport and produced a book about Alpine climbing called *The Playground of Europe*. It is still regarded as a classic statement of the mountaineer's attitude.

In being a scholar and an aesthete—as well as a man of some wealth and social standing—Stephen was highly representative of the British climbers of this period. In fact, during the Golden Age, mountain climbing was, perforce, strictly an upper class sport. The cost involved in mounting an Alpine expedition made it impossible for any but men of means and leisure.

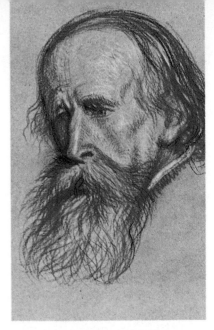

Above: Leslie Stephen, the English scholar and philosopher who became a passionate devotee of mountaineering. Below: title page and frontispiece of his book, considered the classic statement of the mountaineer's attitude.

ASCENT OF THE ROTHHORN.

THE

PLAYGROUND OF EUROPE.

BY

LESLIE STEPHEN,

LATE PRESIDENT OF THE ALPINE CLUB.

VALLEY OF LAUTERBRUNNEN.

'We complain of the mountains as rubbish, as not only disfiguring the face of the earth, but also to us useless and inconvenient; and yet, without these, neither rivers nor fountains nor the weather for producing and ripening fruits could regularly be produced.'

Abp. KING *On the Origin of Evil.*

LONDON:
LONGMANS, GREEN, AND CO.
1871.

Above: as mountaineering increased in popularity, a good many Swiss took advantage of their local knowledge and became guides. Several grew quite famous for their daring climbs. This photograph of a group of guides was taken in Zermatt by the Victorian mountain photographer G. P. Abraham.

One of the gentleman climber's chief expenses was the services of professional guides. Although, later on, many mountaineers began climbing without guides, it was at first thought essential to enlist the aid of local men who possessed not only strength and skill, but also a thorough knowledge of mountain terrain and weather conditions. Most of the professional guides of the period were Swiss peasants, one-time herdsmen or chamois-hunters. A good many of them loved mountains and mountain climbing as much as their employers, and more than a few earned themselves an honored place in the history of the sport. Their vital importance to the success of a climb was fully recognized and acknowledged by the amateurs who employed them, and there often grew up between amateur and guide a deep-felt bond of fellowship. The comradeship between guide and amateur early became one of the traditions of the sport.

Of the many leading Swiss guides of the period, one of the best-known was Christian Almer. Born in Grindelwald in 1826, Almer did not begin his climbing career until he was about 28, when he joined Alfred Wills' Wetterhorn ascent party. Two years later he became a professional guide. In the next few years, he took part in many first ascents, including that of the Grandes Jorasses (13,806 feet) near Mont Blanc, and that of the Eiger (13,040 feet) in the

Right: one of the best known of these Swiss guides was Christian Almer. This photograph of him, with his wife Margharitha, was taken just after they had climbed the Wetterhorn to celebrate their 50th wedding anniversary.

Below: Melchior Anderegg, another of the Alpine guides active during the Golden Age, who gained international fame for his superb climbing skill.

Bernese Alps. The famed British climber Edward Whymper once wrote of him that "There is not a truer heart or a surer foot to be found amongst the Alps." Almer was a vigorous and enthusiastic climber to the end of his days. In 1896, he and his devoted wife Margharitha climbed the Wetterhorn to celebrate their Golden Wedding Anniversary. He was then 70 and she 72.

Another well-known Swiss guide of the mid-1800's was Melchior Anderegg, born in 1827. Anderegg began his career as a herdsman, chamois-hunter, and wood-carver. His first opportunity to serve as a guide came when he was in his early 20's, and from then on, mountain climbing became his life. He was Leslie Stephen's favorite guide, and made many first ascents with him. Another distinguished mountaineer with whom he worked was a woman, Lucy Walker. Anderegg was her guide on climbs over a 20-year period and, inevitably, she fell in love with him. Asked why she had never married, she once said, "I love mountains and Melchior, and Melchior already has a wife." Whymper, one of the many other mountaineers who employed Anderegg at one time or another, valued him as highly as he did Almer. "Melchior," he said, "is a very prince among guides."

Guides played a vital part in every major ascent of the Golden

Age. But perhaps in no case was their role so crucial—or so controversial—as in the dramatic episode that marked the end of the decade. This was Edward Whymper's ascent of the Matterhorn, a climb that began with a rivalry, ended in a tragic disaster, and became a legend in its own time.

Born in 1840, Edward Whymper began his career as an apprentice in his father's wood-engraving business, and soon became a master craftsman. At the age of 20, he was commissioned to illustrate the Alpine Club's first series of books, *Peaks, Passes, and Glaciers*. It was this task that first brought him face to face with the Matterhorn.

Situated in the Pennine Alps, the Matterhorn rises to a height of 14,685 feet on the Italian-Swiss border near the town of Zermatt.

Left: the Eiger and Mönsch, painted in watercolor by Edward Whymper, an artist who discovered mountaineering through a commission to illustrate an Alpine Club publication. He became one of those climbers who develop an obsession about a specific mountain — in his case, it was the Matterhorn.

It is neither the highest nor the most difficult mountain in the Alps, but its four sharp ridges, ending in a peaked summit that seems to overhang its own slopes, give it a forbidding and inaccessible appearance. It is often topped with a plume of billowing cloud that signals the onset of a storm in its upper reaches.

Whymper was not immediately impressed by the towering beauty of this mighty peak. Indeed, his first reaction, as he recorded it in his diary, was to feel contempt for all the writers—Ruskin in particular—who had penned "such precious stuff" about the mountain. This reaction was typical of Whymper, who all his life was an independent, stubborn, and opinionated man.

But if he felt no awe of the mountain, Whymper at once felt a strong ambition to master it. At first he might simply have meant to

Above: the Matterhorn, for years considered impossible to climb, which came to be so important in the history and legend of Alpine mountaineering.

Above: Luc Meynet, a little hunchback who overcame his disability to go high in the mountains. He climbed with Edward Whymper on many occasions, but did not take part in the dramatic ascent to the summit of the Matterhorn.

"knock" the growing mystique surrounding alpinism, but once he had formed his resolve to conquer the Matterhorn, it became the dominating factor in his life. His determination to be the first man on its summit drove him to make no fewer than seven attempts between 1861 and 1864.

Whymper was not the only man who wanted to conquer the Matterhorn. A number of other climbers had also begun making attempts. Of these, the only man with as fixed a resolve as Whymper's was an Italian patriot named Jean-Antoine Carrel. Born in 1829 in a little village at the very foot of the Matterhorn, Carrel was determined that the honor of its first ascent should go to an Italian. When, therefore, Whymper began his series of attempts on the summit, Carrel was deeply resentful of the young Englishman. Whymper, however, seems to have been unaware of this, and sought to join forces with the Italian for yet another attempt on the mountain in 1865.

Carrel went so far as to sign up for Whymper's 1865 expedition, but his patriotism was far stronger than any contract. When an Italian party showed up a few days before Whymper's departure and announced their plan of beating the Englishman to the top, Carrel immediately joined them.

Carrel's defection enraged Whymper. For four years the young Englishman had launched repeated assaults on the mountain. Time after time it had defeated him, but he had felt sure that *this* time, particularly with the help of the one man who knew the Matterhorn even better than he himself, he would succeed. But now! Not only were the members of the Italian team blessed with the services of Carrel; they were also superbly equipped and skilled in the most advanced climbing techniques. Worse still, Whymper could find no one willing to join him—even the great-hearted little hunchback guide Luc Keynet, Whymper's loyal companion on earlier attempts, was engaged elsewhere. At the beginning of July, Edward Whymper found himself without an expedition and in danger of losing his coveted prize—the glory of conquering the Matterhorn—to a team of well-prepared rivals.

Yet Whymper refused to be daunted, and within two weeks he was able to assemble an ascent party of seven men. The first to join

MICHEL A. CROZ.

Hadow.

Charles Hudson 1828-1865

Lord F. Douglas 1847-65

Peter Taugwalder-Vater

1865 (22)
Peter Taugwalder-Sohn

Above: photographs of the members of Whymper's party who finally set out to conquer the Matterhorn. In the top row, left to right, Michel Croz, Douglas Hadow, Charles Hudson, and Lord Francis Douglas; lower row, Peter Taugwalder senior, Edward Whymper, and the younger Peter Taugwalder.

Left: the letter in which the guide Michel-Auguste Croz originally refused Whymper's invitation to join his attempt to conquer the Matterhorn. Croz was killed during the descent.

43

him was the youthful but experienced English climber Lord Francis Douglas. Douglas was accompanied by his guide, Peter Taugwalder, and by Peter's father, the highly skilled guide Peter Taugwalder senior. Two experienced mountaineers and two good guides were the making of an expedition. And, on the very day that young Peter's father agreed to join the party, Whymper had another stroke of luck.

In his original plans, Whymper had been counting on Michel-Auguste Croz, one of the most expert and sought-after guides of the period. Croz had had to withdraw early on, but now he returned to Zermatt in the employ of the Reverend Charles Hudson, a veteran alpinist, who was also bent on the conquest of the Matterhorn. The two parties joined forces. Hudson was accompanied by a 19-year-old novice climber named Douglas Hadow. Later, Whymper was to claim that he had opposed the inclusion of the youth. Certainly it was hazardous to take a beginner on a climb regarded as one of the Alps' most perilous. However, Hudson had promised his young companion that they would attempt the Matterhorn, and it was probably on his insistence that Hadow was made one of the party.

The climb began on the morning of July 13, 1865 with Whymper and Hudson leading. The ascent of the lower slopes of the ridge was free of incident, and the party camped that night within 3,000 feet of the summit. "Long after dusk," Whymper wrote later, "the cliffs above echoed with our laughter and with the songs of the guides, for we were happy and feared no evil." The precipices of the steep east face still lay before them, but Croz, who had reconnoitered the route before dusk, had reported that they presented no real difficulty. The climbers had ample reason to be in good spirits.

The next morning they set out early and, within a few hours, Whymper and Croz were racing triumphantly up the final ridge of the great peak. At this point, Whymper was still not absolutely sure that he might not yet be beaten to the summit by Carrel. The Italian party had set out before his own and, although they would be slowed down by the heavy gear they were carrying, they might just possibly snatch the victory from him.

A few hundred feet from the summit, Whymper and Croz unroped from the others and made a dash for the highest point. As they neared the top, Whymper, obsessed with the fear that Carrel might have been there before him, anxiously scanned the snow on the summit ahead. There was not a footstep to be seen! He looked down: yes, there was Carrel and his party, still struggling up the south face, hundreds of yards below him. He let out a whoop of delight and, with Croz, rolled a few rocks down the face to signal his victory to his rival.

After they had set up a flag (seen both in Zermatt and in Breuil, where the villagers confidently believed that it was the sign of an Italian victory), the party rested on the summit for nearly an hour. Then, at 2:40 P.M., they began the descent. No doubt the men were exhausted and over excited by their triumph. In any case, they were

Above: the triumphant success, as visualized by the French artist Gustave Doré, as Edward Whymper stands at the summit of his mountain.

Right: disaster struck as the climbers began their jubilant descent. Doré pictures the moment of horror as the fall occurs. On the lower end of the rope is Croz, then Hadow—whose slip caused the fall—the Rev. Hudson, and above him Lord Francis Douglas. Old Peter Taugwalder tenses his body as the rope snaps in two, and those below him on the rope fall to their deaths.

Left: a photograph of Hadow's flimsy and inadequate boot. It was studded with flat-headed nails, and had smooth iron tips round the heels. Douglas Hadow was an inexperienced climber, and his role in the tragedy has often been argued in the search for the cause of Alpine mountaineering's most famous accident.

Below: another subject for controversy has been the ropes used on the ascent of the Matterhorn, pictured below. The one which broke is shown on the left. It was known as the stout sash line.

much less cautious on the way down than they had been on the way up, and they had not gone far before they met with tragedy.

Croz was leading the descent with Hadow immediately following him. Hudson and Lord Francis Douglas came next, with "old" Peter Taugwalder, his son, and Whymper himself bringing up the rear. Roped together, they began moving down the jutting shoulder of rock that had given them their only moment of difficulty on the ascent. Croz was helping Hadow by actually placing the young man's feet in position, step by step. Suddenly, Hadow slipped, and fell against Croz, knocking him off balance. Caught unawares, Hudson and Douglas were dragged down by the falling weight of their companions. Higher up, the three others braced themselves to take the strain as the rope went taut. But the shock never came. The rope spinning out between Douglas and Taugwalder held for only a fraction of a second—and then broke. The four men plunged to their deaths thousands of feet below as the two Taugwalders and Whymper looked on in stunned disbelief.

The three remaining members of the party were too shattered to move for over half an hour. When at last they did begin the descent to Zermatt, it was in a state of shock and near hysteria.

The tremendous publicity given to the Matterhorn disaster led to

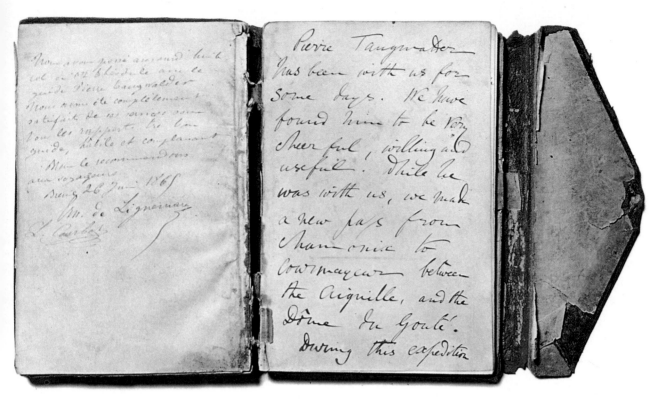

Pierre Taugwalder has been with us for some days. We have found him to be very cheerful, willing and useful. While he was with us, we made a new pass from Chamonix to Courmayeur between the Aiguille, and the Dôme du Goûté. During this expedition

Above: all the mountain guides kept reference books, in which clients wrote recommendations. This is young Peter Taugwalder's book. The Matterhorn climb is missing, since his client, Lord Francis Douglas, was killed and unable to provide him with the usual reference.

widespread condemnation of the sport in England. Queen Victoria even went so far as to make inquiries about whether mountain climbing could be prohibited by law. But even greater than the disapproval it aroused was the controversy generated by the Matterhorn tragedy. Who was to blame?

The responsibility for the disaster has not and never will be finally settled. Immediately after the event, it was rumored that Peter Taugwalder senior had actually cut the rope to save himself from being dragged down with the others. But even at the time, men doubted whether any climber could have acted quickly enough to sever the rope—particularly in such a way that it would appear to have broken of its own accord as it went taut. Far more damaging was the discovery that the rope used on the descent was old and

Right: the graves of Charles Hudson and Douglas Hadow, two of the victims of the accident which brought to a close the Golden Age of climbing.

The Alps have traditionally been known for their hot water springs which have also attracted tourists. This woodcut shows the spa of Leukerbad, which was so hot that a traveler in 1544 noted it was possible to boil eggs in it.

weak and had been intended only as a reserve. In fact, the party had had with them several coils of sound rope, and both guides came under fire for the decision—if decision it was—to use the weaker rope. The ultimate responsibility for checking the party's equipment before the descent, of course, rested with Whymper as leader of the expedition. Nevertheless, it was not Whymper, but old Taugwalder whose reputation suffered. In fact, the "Lion of Zermatt," as Peter Taugwalder senior was called, never made another great Alpine climb after the Matterhorn. Instead, he spent the rest of his life outside Europe altogether, climbing in Greenland and the Andes.

The Golden Age came to an end with the fatal Matterhorn assault, but not entirely as a result of the tragedy. By this time, mountaineers had climbed nine-tenths of the Alpine peaks—peaks that had remained virgin since the mountains themselves were born. It was only natural that, as the number of remaining "firsts" dwindled, the great dawn of Alpine climbing should draw to a close.

But despite the fact that all the great peaks and many of the lesser ones had been scaled, and despite the sensation caused by the Matterhorn disaster, the popularity of mountaineering continued to race ahead. The next few decades saw a boom in the Swiss tourist industry as more and more men and women traveled to the Alps to climb. For a time, the British kept their lead in Alpine mountaineering, but soon that lead was being challenged by distinguished climbers from many other countries—Switzerland, France, Germany, Austria, and Italy. Non-European mountaineers, too, began to make a name for themselves in the Alps. And indeed, one of the most famous Alpine climbers after the Golden Age was an American, William Augustus Brevoort Coolidge.

Coolidge was not the first American to climb in the Alps, but he was the first American to gain a worldwide mountaineering reputation. Born in New York in 1850, Coolidge was frail and sickly as a child. Doctors recommended mountain air to improve his health and, when he was 14, his devoted aunt, Marguerite Brevoort, took him across the Atlantic to travel in the Alps. The pair embarked on a series of energetic Alpine walks, which became increasingly adventurous as young Coolidge gained in strength and vigor. From these walks it was but a short step to real mountaineering, and in the next few years the two took on greater and greater challenges. Marguerite, "the great Dutch-American miss," as a Swiss contemporary called

All mountaineering was not a serious undertaking. The Alps became attractive to tourists desiring an easy visit to high places. This engraving shows a party on the mountain. Such efforts were called "salon mountaineering."

Queen Margherita of Italy climbed the Monte Rosa in 1893 so that she might be present at the opening of the Capanna Margherita, the highest Alpine hut for the shelter of climbers. The photograph shows the queen and her party, the women wearing face masks to protect their skin from the sun, as a suntan was unseemly for a lady.

her, became the first woman to scale the Matterhorn. And Coolidge, who never returned to America and liked to consider himself a British climber, went on to make no fewer than 600 major ascents. In so doing, he became one of the finest alpinists of his day, and won the accolade of being made an honorary member of the British Alpine Club, a privilege granted to few non-British climbers at that time.

By the last quarter of the century, the Alps had been well and truly tamed. What had once been historic achievements were now standard climbs. Even the Matterhorn might be climbed scores of

times in a single season. For the average amateur the "standard" climbs were sufficiently demanding and rewarding. But for the most expert devotees, something more was needed, some new challenge. With no virgin Alpine summits left to conquer, skilled mountaineers increasingly turned to two new avenues of adventure. One was the conquest of unclimbed peaks elsewhere in the world. The other was the conquest of "impossible" routes and faces in the Alps themselves. The mountaineers who took up this latter challenge made "the route, not the summit," the object of their endeavors. In so doing, they ultimately changed the entire character of alpinism.

New Routes and New Techniques

4

The pioneering of new routes to Alpine summits began as early as 1865, the year of the Matterhorn disaster. In that year, the British mountaineer A. W. Moore climbed to the top of Mont Blanc by way of the Brenva ice-ridge, a far more difficult approach to the summit than that taken by Paccard and De Saussure. In 1877, an even more arduous ascent of Mont Blanc's south face was made by J. Eccles, who reached the top by way of the treacherous Brouillard and Frêney glaciers.

One of the foremost exponents of the "new route" school of mountaineering was Albert Frederick Mummery. He is considered by many to be the founder of this school. Certainly, his example had a profound influence on the whole generation of climbers after the Golden Age. Bold, even reckless in some of his exploits, Mummery nevertheless laid strong emphasis on mountaineering technique, and was one of the first alpinists to climb without guides.

During his long mountaineering career, Mummery pioneered new routes in almost every district of the Alps. Chief among his achievements was his ascent of the Matterhorn's perilous Zmutt Ridge in 1879 and his scaling of the north face of the Grépon (11,423 feet) in 1881. The latter climb, as well as his ascent of Mont Blanc's Brenva Ridge, was made without guides.

Another adventurous pioneer of new routes during this period was Clinton Dent. Of the many assaults he made on difficult Alpine faces, perhaps none was so remarkable as his ascent of the Grand Dru (12,316 feet) in 1878. The sheer face of this peak makes its summit almost unattainable; Dent himself succeeded only after 18 attempts.

Both Dent and Mummery were adept at rock climbing, a mountaineering skill the importance of which came to be fully realized only after the Golden Age. Before the 1870's, most alpinists—though skilled at maneuvering on ice—tended to shy away from rock climbs. Faced with a choice between a short rocky route and a longer, ice-clad route to a summit, they would almost always choose the icy one, even if it meant spending hours hacking out steps in the

Left: Layton Kor, Dougal Haston, and John Harlin standing below the North Face of the Eiger, and spread out in front of them the vast battery of equipment required for them to attempt this most challenging of modern climbs.

Above: Mummery scaling the Crack on the north face of the Grepon. He was the first man to make this climb and went up wearing a white shirt and carrying a rope which was simply looped around his waist.

Above: as the part that rock climbing played in Alpine climbs became more obvious, many climbers took advantage of the mountainous regions of Britain before trying the higher Alpine peaks. This picture was taken in the 1870's.

ice. In fact, one of the reasons why the Matterhorn was not climbed until 1865 was because its ascent entailed so much rock climbing.

But the mountaineer's attitude toward Alpine rock faces changed radically in the decades that followed the Golden Age. The change was due in part to the exploits of men such as Mummery and Dent, in part to the growth of a new sport, and in part to the development of new equipment.

Above: a modern rock climber negotiates a rock overhang in Malham Cove, in England's Yorkshire region. He wears a helmet for protection from falling rock and sits in nylon slings held to the cliff by karabiners attached to pitons in the rock. This sort of sophisticated equipment enables him to make climbs his Victorian counterpart could not possibly have contemplated.

The new sport was rock climbing itself. In the 1870's in Britain, increasing numbers of climbers began traveling to the mountainous regions of Scotland, North Wales, and the Lake District to practice and improve their climbing skills in preparation for later Alpine assaults. Even the highest of Britain's peaks, Ben Nevis (4,406 feet), is lowly by Alpine standards. Nevertheless, the Welsh and Scottish peaks, together with the rocky pinnacles of the Lake District, offer a multitude of taxing and varied climbing problems. This was soon discovered by the men and women who scaled them for practice in the 1870's and 1880's. As they perfected the special rope and balancing techniques required on rock ridges and faces, they found themselves developing a whole new branch of mountaineering. Rock climbing soon came to be recognized as a sport in its own right, and became increasingly popular, not only in Britain, but elsewhere in Europe as well.

It was not long before ardent rock climbers who had mastered all the difficult pinnacles in their own countries were traveling to the Alps to test their skills against the more severe challenges of the rock faces there. The perils of scaling an Alpine peak via a wall of rock are infinitely greater than those of any "standard" Alpine climb. But the mountaineers for whom the route, not the summit, was the objective, were undeterred by the dangers. Soon, men such as Mummery and Dent were pioneering one "impossible" rock route after another. But if improved rock climbing techniques were vital to the success of these "new route" pioneers, so also were the innovations in climbing equipment that came thick and fast in the decades after the Golden Age.

In the early days of Alpine mountaineering, men had assailed the heights armed only with the most basic and primitive climbing aids: long, pointed walking-sticks called *alpenstocks; crampons* to give a surer footing on ice; axes for cutting steps in the ice; and rope for linking the members of a party together. One of the first improvements was the development of the ice-ax, which replaced both the alpenstock and the common ax carried by early mountaineers. Three feet long, the ice-ax has a spike at one end. The other end has a metal head, pointed on one side and adz-shaped on the other. The climber can use the ice-ax as an anchor by driving its spiked end into ice or rock and securing his rope to it. In this way, rope and ice-ax have arrested—and prevented—many a fall. Rope and ice-ax have also been used in combination countless times in the rescue of climbers who have had the terrifying experience of crashing down into the well of a hidden crevasse.

In the early decades of the 1900's, another new piece of mountaineering equipment was developed specifically for rock climbers. This was the *piton*, a metal spike eight inches long with a hole at one end. The spike can be driven into the narrowest of cracks in the rock and a rope passed through the hole to give the safety of a belay where the face offers no natural projection around which to fasten a safety rope. The piton can itself be used as a foothold, or serve as a hook from which to hang a rope foothold, or stirrup, called an *étrier*. In some cases the étrier is a simple sling of rope; in others it is a miniature rope ladder with three wooden rungs. But in all cases, it is secured to the hole in the protruding end of the piton by a metal *karabiner*, or snap-link. Using pitons, snap-links, and a make-shift hammock, the climber may even spend the night on a sheer face of rock.

Even when there are no cracks in the rock face into which pitons can be driven, the climber may still continue the ascent if he has either a "sky-hook" (a form of metal claw which can give a purchase on even the most minute protrusion in the rock), or expansion bolts. To use the latter, the climber must drill a hole in the rock, insert a hollow metal sleeve, and then screw in a threaded piton.

Below: a hunting scene of the 1400's. Left: a detail from the picture showing possibly one of the earliest climbers to use a rope for a safe descent from a rock outcropping.

Right: use of pitons and karabiners on a rock face. A nylon rope has been threaded through the karabiner which is clipped to a piton that has been driven firmly into a crack in the rock.

Far right: Rusty Baillie, an American climber, is shown jumaring, a method of climbing a rope hanging free from the rock face. The picture was taken on the east face of the Old Man of Hoy, a sheer rock pillar in Scotland.

Pitons and expansion bolts enable modern rock climbers to gain hundreds of feet on "impossible" faces, but they do have drawbacks. If the party takes enough of them to cover the whole route up the face, the sheer weight of metal to be carried becomes a formidable handicap. If, on the other hand, each peg and bolt is withdrawn after use, valuable time—and energy—is lost. Still, without these artificial aids, many a near-vertical wall of rock would never have been scaled. It is interesting to note in passing, the conventions surrounding the use of artificial aids. Even today mountaineers would not dream of cutting steps in the rock, much less of actually erecting a fixed scaffold against a difficult face. Yet a battery of pegs and bolts may be driven into a rock face to make an ascent possible where there are no natural holds. The conventions seem inconsistent to the layman, but are clearly understood and accepted by the devotee.

Another major advance in climbing equipment during this century has been the development of nylon rope. It is lighter than hempen rope, does not freeze at high altitudes, and has great elasticity, which reduces the danger of internal injury when a serious fall is arrested by the jerk of the rope. Nylon and the other man-made fibers used in today's mountaineering gear—tents, clothing, and sleeping bags— give the modern climber a tremendous advantage over his predecessors.

Victorian climbers might well have welcomed the development of lighter, warmer clothing and more flexible rope. But they would have been aghast at the elaborate mechanical equipment used by the modern climber. In the early days, mountaineers refused to use any artificial aids that modified the structure of the mountainside. The sole exception to this rule was the cutting of ice-steps. (In the Victorian view, the ice could not reasonably be considered a part of the mountain itself, and could therefore be "modified" with impunity).

As in most things, so in mountaineering, the approach of the younger generation is despised by its elders and its methods regarded as a betrayal of the true faith. In the late 1800's, Mummery, Dent,

Above: a group of climbers during the mid-1800's, roped together. Notice the very short lengths of rope between the climbers—only about six feet—and that the man on the extreme left has the rope tied round his wrist. In case of his companions falling he would be unable to hold them with the rope as it is shown secured here.

and the other pioneers of new routes and the sport of rock climbing were criticized for their "rock gymnastics." And, in the early 1900's, when almost all the "justifiable" Alpine faces had been conquered, and only the most terrifying ascent route remained virgin, the heroic men who tackled them were accused of "suicidal madness." Moreover, when they began to use pitons as the only way to broach these formidable walls, they were criticized for employing "engineering" tactics.

By the 1930's, there were only three great Alpine rock walls that had not yet been conquered. One of these was the north face of the Matterhorn—4,000 feet of ledgeless, crumbling rock. It was first conquered in the summer of 1931 by two young Germans, Franz and Toni Schmid and, as recently as 1953, was the scene of a remarkable solo ascent by the Italian climber, Walter Bonatti. The second of these three formidable rock faces was the north face of the Grandes Jorasses in the Mont Blanc region. An even more difficult climb than the north wall of the Matterhorn, the rock face of the Grandes Jorasses was first mastered in 1935 by Martin Meir and Rudolf Peters.

The third of these "impossible" rock faces, perhaps the most

Above: modern climbers on a mountain. The emphasis has changed to greater safety as mountaineering has become more and more difficult. Notice the length of rope between the climbers—long enough so that each can act independently, and yet offer an anchor should his companion slip. To provide the most stable hold, each has the rope looped around his body.

Right: a pair of climbing boots with crampons attached. By biting into a snowy or icy surface, crampons enable a climber to move comparatively easily.

awesome precipice in the whole of the Alps, was the Eigerwand, the North Face of the Eiger in the Bernese Alps. From other approaches, the mountain itself (13,040 feet) presents no great difficulties. But the Eigerwand approach was for a long time thought to be impossible. The editor of the *Alpine Journal* once described it as "an obsession for the mentally deranged."

The Eigerwand begins at a point some 3,000 feet from the summit and plunges down almost vertically for 6,000 feet. By modern standards, the technical problems of the route are not great, but the conditions on the face in all but the best weather are lethal. Falling rocks and avalanches of ice thunder down the mountainside at frequent intervals; cutting winds, snow squalls, and hail storms are liable to spring up at any moment; rain or melt-water can suddenly freeze on the rock, turning the surface into a wall of glass. These are the factors which have made the north wall of the Eiger one of the most notorious climbs in the world.

Before it was first conquered, in 1938, the Eigerwand claimed eight lives. Four of these tragic deaths occurred on a single climb in 1936—a climb that began with high hopes and ended with one of the most heart-rending dramas in the annals of mountaineering.

The team consisted of Andreas Hinterstoisser, Willy Angerer, Edi Rainer, and Toni Kurz. All four were seasoned climbers, and all four were determined to succeed. The Olympic Games were being held in Berlin that summer and Adolf Hitler himself had promised that the first climbers to conquer the Eigerwand would be rewarded with gold medals.

The first stages of the ascent went well. Using fingers and toes, ropes and pitons, the four worked their way up from one tiny crevice to another, undaunted by the menacing overhangs and almost vertical sections of smooth rock they encountered. By the morning of the third day, they were within 1,000 feet of their goal. But the weather was worsening rapidly. Snow, hail, rain, and melt-water began to stream down the face and soon froze on the rock, making a treacherous surface of *verglas*. Further progress upward became impossible. The team had no choice but to give up the attempt and begin their retreat. But already the surface of the face

Above: yet another challenge which a few climbers set for themselves is solo climbing. Here Walter Bonatti makes his solo assault on the north face of the Matterhorn, facing 4,000 feet of ledgeless, crumbling rock alone.

had become so wet and glassy that it was as dangerous to move downward as it was to go up. Within a very short time, the four were brought to a complete standstill. They were trapped high up on the face on an exposed section of rock.

Far below, their ascent had been anxiously watched through telescopes. Fear had clutched at the hearts of the watchers when they saw the rain and snow begin to pour down the face. Through the swirling mists they saw the four climbers start to descend, then come to a halt. A rescue party was organized at once, but few believed that it would be able to reach the men while the condition of the face remained so treacherous. Ascending the mountain via the Jungfrau Railway tunnel (which bores right through the Eiger), the rescue team emerged on the outer face about 300 feet below the stranded men. Suddenly, as they began the dangerous traverse toward them, the rescuers heard an agonized cry from above: "Help! The others are all dead—I'm the only one left. Help!"

It was 23-year-old Toni Kurz. Rainer had died of exposure; Hinterstoisser had fallen to his death; and Angerer had been fatally injured by the pull of the rope as his companion fell. Kurz, too, was injured. He was also severely frostbitten and almost at the end of his reserves of strength. Yet he hung on, as the rescue team toiled slowly upward. But a mere 100 feet from him they were stopped by a sheer, ice-covered overhang of rock. They could not get to him; he must somehow get down to them. Following their instructions, he managed to lengthen his own rope with sections from those of his companions. On this rope, a makeshift sling, together with pitons and a hammer, were passed up to him. All this took several hours, but at last, slowly and painfully, he began to lower himself toward his rescuers. Above them in the gathering darkness, they could hear his ice-covered boots scraping against the wall as he moved downward in perilous jerks. Suddenly a knot in the long life-line jammed in one of the snap-links. With his last strength he strove to force it through, but it would not go. Frantically, the rescue team shouted encouragement to him, but Kurz could do no more, and there, only a few feet from safety, the brave young man collapsed and died.

At last, in 1938, the Eigerwand was conquered by another German-Austrian team, consisting of Fritz Kasparek, Heinrich Harrer, Ludwig Vörg, and Andreas Heckmair. Since then, the Eiger's North Face has been scaled a number of times. One of the

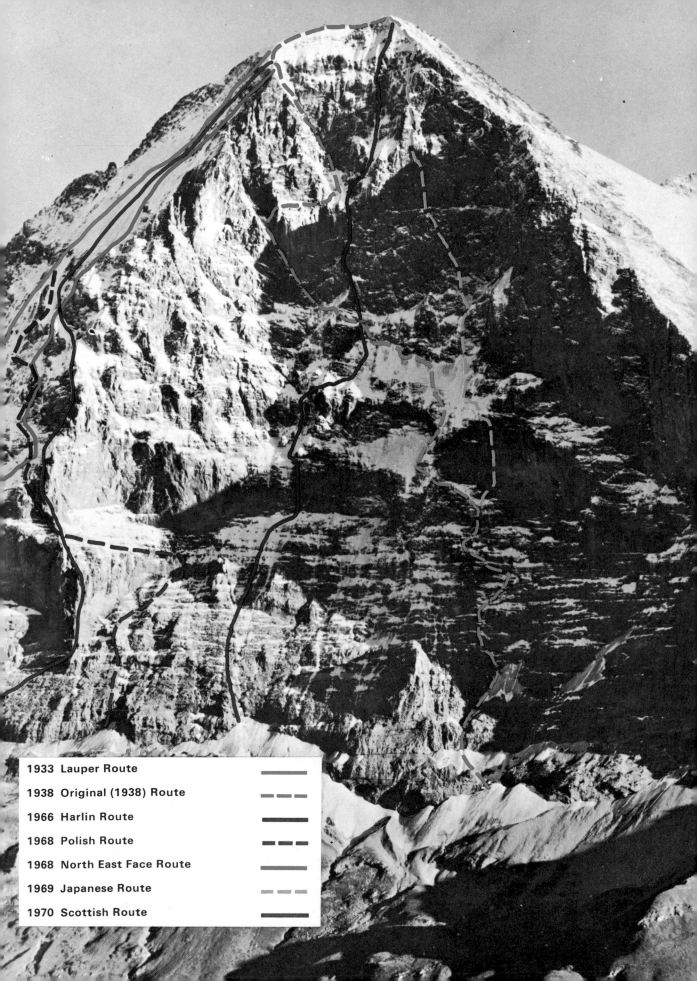

1933 Lauper Route	——————
1938 Original (1938) Route	– – – – –
1966 Harlin Route	——————
1968 Polish Route	– – – –
1968 North East Face Route	——————
1969 Japanese Route	– – – – –
1970 Scottish Route	——————

Above: John Harlin in a helicopter flying low over the Eiger's North Face to survey the uncharted sections of an unclimbed route, the *direttissima*. Harlin was killed during the climb.

Left: Dougal Haston, his face covered with ice, at the summit of the Eiger. Originally a member of the party with Harlin, he joined a German party and went on to complete the assault after the fatal accident.

Right: the North Face of the Eiger has maintained its fascination for climbers of all nations, as one of the most challenging of all climbs, demanding great skill and almost perfect weather for success. Here Chris Bonington, who conquered the face in 1962, stands in front of the Eiger.

most notable of these assaults was that led by the brilliant American climber John Harlin in 1966. It was Harlin's plan to scale the face by the *direttissima,* or direct route. It was an extremely hazardous route, but all went well until the party was within 2,000 feet of the summit. Then, without warning, Harlin's rope broke and he fell to his death. Rather than abandon the climb for which Harlin had given his life, his companion, Dougal Haston, then joined forces with a German party of four that was making the ascent by the ordinary route. Together, the five men reached the summit by the *direttissima,* which they named the John Harlin Route.

Chris Bonington, one of the finest climbers of modern times, made the first British ascent of the Eigerwand in 1962. He has stated that the North Face of the Eiger is now a "justifiable" ascent—but only for those climbers who have proved their skill, determination, and endurance on such faces as the north wall of the Matterhorn and the north wall of the Grandes Jorasses. The Eigerwand is still one of the most formidable climbing problems in the world.

Below: Lenin Peak. In Russia climbing is organized with prizes, proficiency ratings, and penalties. Here mountaineers from the Soviet Union, Poland, and seven other countries gather for a joint climbing expedition.

The same impulse that drove some men to seek out ever more difficult routes and faces in the Alps, drove others to seek still-virgin summits elsewhere in the world. And, as more and more of the great Alpine peaks were conquered, more and more mountaineers traveled to faraway ranges to find challenge and adventure.

The first major European mountaineering expedition outside the Alps took place in the Russian Caucasus in 1868. This rugged range, generally considered to be the dividing line between Europe and Asia, stretches from northwest to southeast for some 750 miles between the Black and Caspian Seas. The 1868 expedition was led by the British alpinist and geographer Douglas Freshfield, and included two well-known English climbers, A. W. Moore and C. C. Tucker. As the Caucasus were at that time virtually unknown to Western climbers, the three men spent much of their time simply exploring and mapping the peaks and valleys of the range. Nevertheless, they did make the first ascents to a number of peaks, including Kazbek (16,545 feet) and the lower of the twin summits of Elbrus. (The other of Elbrus' two summits, some 18,481 feet high, was not climbed until 1874.) Freshfield's party was assisted by the local Urusbieh guides, whose skill and toughness greatly impressed them. Indeed, it would seem that these upland tribesmen were by no means inexperienced climbers themselves, for the Englishmen recorded that they were already familiar with a type of crampon.

The next major expedition to the Caucasus was in 1886 when Clinton Dent and W. F. Donkin, accompanied by the well-known Alpine guide Alexander Burgener, scaled Gestola, a peak some

Below: Prince Naurus of Urusbieh with some of his family. His subjects impressed the members of the first expedition to the Caucasus by their climbing ability.

16,000 feet in height. Two years later, Donkin and Dent visited the Caucasus again. On this occasion they were accompanied by a third British climber, Henry Fox. Toward the end of August Donkin and Fox set out from a camp on the Ullauz Glacier to make an attempt on the forbidding heights of Koshtantau (16,875 feet). They were never seen again. For a year there was no news of their fate; rumor had it that they had been waylaid by bandits. But in 1889, a search party led by Douglas Freshfield found their last camp intact; everything was in order and there was no sign of foul play. Although their bodies were never found, it was clear that the men had lost their lives somewhere in the heights of the great mountain they had tried to conquer. In 1887, another expedition did succeed in reaching the summit of Koshtantau, and in 1888, A. F. Mummery scaled the second highest peak in the range, Dykhtau (17,050 feet). In the remaining decades before the outbreak of World War I, many other peaks in the Caucasus range were climbed for the first time.

The highest mountains in Asia, apart from the Himalaya, are the Pamirs of the Soviet Union. In fact, they are sometimes classified as a north-western extension of the Himalayan system. Of the many lofty summits in this Soviet range, Kaufman Peak (23,382 feet) was for a long time thought to be the highest. It was first climbed in 1928 by a Russo-German team led by the German mountaineer W. R. Rickmers. This was a heroic accomplishment—the first complete ascent of a peak over 23,000 feet since 1907. And to celebrate the achievement, the Russians renamed the mountain Lenin Peak.

But four years after this ascent, another peak in the Pamirs was found to be over 1,000 feet higher than Lenin Peak. Stalin Peak (24,590 feet), as the new monarch of the range was named, is situated, like Lenin Peak, in the Tadzhikistan. Skirted by a large glacier, it is one of the world's most beautiful mountains. But its ascent is fraught with terrible hazards, and the Soviet team that first

Above: Russian mountaineers climb over a snow-capped ridge. Climbs once considered difficult are now made annually by large parties of young men and women, as part of a carefully graded series of mountain trials.

Left: high on the slopes of Koshtantau, the abandoned bivouac of Donkin and Fox was found by a search party in 1889. When they failed to return from their attempt on the peak, it was thought that they had been waylaid by bandits.

Above: a group of climbers raise the
Soviet flag at the top of Communism
Peak. First climbed in 1933, it
is one of the most beautiful—and most
dangerous—mountains in the world. It
was formerly known as Stalin Peak.

climbed it needed no fewer than eight high camps on the mountain
itself to ensure success.

In 1962, the mountain was again climbed, this time by an Anglo-
Russian party. Since its first ascent in 1932, Stalin Peak's name had
been changed (as part of Krushchev's de-Stalinization program) to
Communism Peak (Pik Kommunisma). Before tackling the great
peak, the expedition climbed a lesser one, Garmo Peak. Here, two
members of the British party, Robin Smith and the great climber
Wilfrid Noyce, fell 4,000 feet to their deaths. But despite the tragedy,
the expedition led jointly by the Russian Anatole Ovchinikov and
the Englishman Sir John Hunt, (now Lord Hunt), went on to climb
Communism Peak. In a book about the climb, one of the party,
Malcolm Slessor, vividly describes the rigors of the climb—the
−20°F temperature, the severe winds and blustering snow squalls,
and the rarified atmosphere that required the climbers to take
several deep breaths before each upward step.

In his account of the expedition, Slessor also touches on a most interesting aspect of Russian mountaineering: its high degree of professionalism. In modern times, mountaineering has been increasingly "professionalized," with many well-known climbs rated on a fixed scale of difficulty. But perhaps nowhere has this process been carried further than in the Soviet Union. The once-arduous ascent of Mount Elbrus is now made every year by large parties of young Russian men and women as one of the lesser trials in a carefully graded series of tests. In the Soviet Union's annual rock-climbing competition, the contestants are required to mark a route on the photograph of an unfamiliar rockface and then scale it without any deviation. Dedicated climbers can win the coveted Master of Sport certificate only after much competition climbing and the step-by-step achievement of various levels of proficiency. Moreover, it is a punishable offense to attempt any climb beyond the level of difficulty a climber has proven himself capable of. In view of the frequent necessity in Western countries of mounting hazardous rescue operations to save novices who have attempted too much, the Russian regulation has much to be said for it. And, in terms of the results achieved, the rigorous training undergone by Soviet mountaineers has some justification. But in the end, however strictly he may have been schooled, the true mountaineer is motivated more by his love of climbing than by any "professional" requirements.

For the mountaineer in Europe, there are, apart from the Alps

Left: the snow-capped summit of Mount Kilimanjaro towers above the plains of Tanzania. An extinct volcano, it is the highest mountain in Africa.

Right: the continent of Africa, showing the mountain ranges and peaks. The highest of Africa's mountains is Kilimanjaro (19,340 feet), situated between Lake Victoria and the Indian Ocean.

Below: the summit of Mount Kilimanjaro. The crater is a mile in diameter, and covered with ice and snow. It is not a difficult climb, and it has been ascended frequently since Meyer first reached the summit in 1889.

EUROPE
10°
20°
Danube
30°
BLACK SEA
40°
ELBRUS
18,481
KAZBEK
16,545
50°
60°
40°
PYRENEES
CORSICA
SARDINIA
MT.
OLYMPUS
9550
MT. PARNASSUS
8061
MT. ETNA
11,122
SICILY
CRETE
CYPRUS
CASPIAN
SEA
MT. ARARAT
16,916
ELBURZ
MT. DEMAVEND
18,934
A
S
I
A
Z A G R O S   M T S.
M E D I T
R R A N E A N   S E A
PERSIAN GULF
TROPIC OF CANCER
30°
Libyan
Desert
Nile
J. MUSA (MT. SINAI)
7400
A r a b i a n
P e n i n s u l a
AHAGGAR
MT. TAHAT
9850
M T S.
L.
Nasser
RED SEA
Rub' al Khali
20°
h a r a
TIBESTI
PIC TOUSSIDE
10,712
MASSIF
EMI KOUSSI
11,204
Nubian
Desert
AIR
Lake
Chad
JEBEL MARRA
MTS.
J. GIMBALA
10,131
Blue Nile
RAS DASHAN
15,158
L. Tana
GULF OF ADEN
SOCOTRA
C. Guardafui
Benue
ABYSSINIAN
HIGHLANDS
BATU
14,131
10°
MT. CAMEROON
13,350
Ubangi
White Nile
Webi Shabele
FERNANDO PÓO
INEA
Congo
PRÍNCIPE
SÃO
TOMÉ
ANNOBÓN
RUWENZORI RA.
MT. STANLEY
16,795
MT. KENYA
17,058
EQUATOR 0°
Congo
Kasai
MILUMBA MTS.
Lake
Victoria
KILIMANJARO
19,340
MERU
14,979
I N D I A N
Lualaba
Lake
Tanganyika
O C E A N
10°
L. Nyasa
L. Malawi
COMORO
IS.
MUCHINGA MTS.
MAROMOKOTRO
9450
Cunene
Cubango
Zambezi
L.
Kariba
UMKWAKWO
MTS.
Namib Desert
Okavango
Basin
MOZAMBIQUE CHANNEL
MADAGASCAR
20°
Kalahari
Desert
Limpopo
TROPIC OF CAPRICORN
Vaal
MT. AUX SOURCES
10,822
Orange
Gt. Karroo
DRAKENSBERG
30°
C. of Good Hope
10°
20°
30°
40°
50°
60°

This label from a can of meat was carried in his pocket by Felice Benuzzi on the amazing first ascent of Lenana. With two fellow Italian prisoners of war, Benuzzi escaped from their prison camp in 1943 to conquer the mountain, taking food they had saved, and improvised tools. Having achieved their goal, they came back and gave themselves up, spending the remainder of the war in captivity.

and the Caucasus, few great peaks to challenge him. Among the beautiful and dramatic mountains of Norway, for example, the highest, Galdhøpiggen, is only 8,097 feet high and offers few difficulties. And Mulhacén (11,424 feet), although it represents the highest point in Spain's Sierra Nevada range, is of even less interest from a mountaineering point of view.

Just across the Strait of Gibraltar rise the Atlas mountains of northern Africa. This range, familiar to the sailors of the ancient world, extends about 1,500 miles through the deserts of northwest Africa and contains a number of substantial peaks, some of which have not yet been climbed. The highest point is Jebel Toubkal (13,661 feet) and is by no means an easy climb.

But for the mountaineer who journeys to Africa, the real challenges lie in the equatorial zone of East Africa. Here, in Tanzania, is found Kilimanjaro (19,340 feet). An extinct volcano, it is the highest mountain in all of Africa and one of the most beautiful in the world. Kilimanjaro's slopes sweep down majestically from its main peak (Kibo) to the lush equatorial forests below, where its mighty glaciers melt and become rushing torrents. The crater at the top of the main peak is more than a mile in diameter and the upper slopes are covered in a coating of ice about 200 feet thick. Kilimanjaro has been climbed many times since its first ascent, in 1889, by the German scientist and mountaineer Hans Meyer.

The next highest mountain in Africa is Mount Kenya, 200 miles north of Kilimanjaro. Although it, too, is of volcanic origin, its slopes are rugged and precipitous. Mount Kenya possesses two main peaks: Batian and Nelion (both about 17,000 feet) and a lesser peak,

Lenana (16,300 feet). When Batian was first scaled by Sir Halford Mackinder in 1899, his party literally had to fight their way over much of the distance against hostile local tribes. Nelion was first climbed 30 years later by another Englishman, Eric Shipton. Mount Kenya's third summit, Lenana, was not conquered until 1943, and the story of that ascent is one of the most remarkable in the annals of mountaineering.

In 1943, three Italian soldiers who were being held in a British prisoner-of-war camp 50 miles from Mount Kenya made up their minds to climb the mountain. Two of them, Felice Benuzzi and Giuan Balleto, were amateur mountaineers, the third, Enzo Barsotti, was a complete novice. Gleaning what knowledge they could about the mountain from what they could see of it and from a book in the camp library, they planned their route. For six months they amassed stores and equipment by saving food and improvising tools. They made anoraks from their camp blankets and crampons from the mudguards of a wrecked van. Then one night, they made their escape from the camp and set off for Mount Kenya. Despite inadequate provisions and equipment and despite the extreme conditions they had to endure—from the tropical heat of the lower slopes to the freezing cold and blizzards near the summit—they achieved their objective. Then the three adventurers made their way back to the British camp and gave themselves up. They had no other alternative, for a complete escape from British-occupied Kenya would have been impossible. But, back in the camp, the three endured their punishment—a few weeks of solitary confinement—without complaint, happy in the knowledge of their remarkable conquest of Lenana.

Thirty-seven years before this daring wartime expedition, another Italian party had conquered Africa's third-highest mountain, Margherita Peak (16,763 feet). This peak is the loftiest point in the Ruwenzori chain of mountains, which lie along the frontier between Uganda and Congo (Kinshasa). The whole chain is sometimes known by its romantic English name, the Mountains of the Moon. Storms and mists habitually cloak the summits of this range, and it was not until 1889, when the American explorer Henry Stanley sighted them, that their full extent was revealed. It has been calculated that rain falls on their slopes for 350 days of the year, and early expeditions were always driven back by the difficulties of toiling through the seemingly endless tropical downpours.

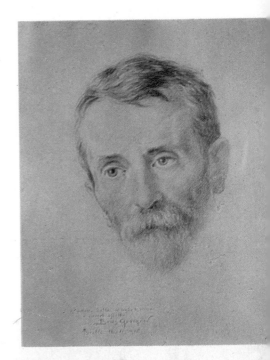

Above: Vittorio Sella, the mountain photographer, who accompanied the Duke of the Abruzzi many times. Below: the camera Sella used in the Caucasus. Earlier, he had an even larger camera, which no longer exists.

71

In 1906, however, the Duke of the Abruzzi, leading one of the finest and most efficiently organized expeditions of all time, succeeded in reaching the summit of Margherita Peak and of the many lesser peaks in the region as well. In the course of the Margherita Peak ascent, the party encountered one of the strangest and most beautiful mountain phenomena in the world. After days of struggle through rain-lashed gorges, the group emerged on the lower slopes to find them covered as far as the eye could see with gigantically enlarged and dazzlingly hued flowers. Before the climb could begin in earnest, the party had to cut their way through this exotic barrier with their axes.

The Duke was accompanied on this expedition, as he was on several others, by the great mountain photographer Vittorio Sella, who brought back many valuable pictures of the Mountains of the Moon. As a whole, the expedition was undertaken with a number of highly scientific objectives in mind. The Duke hoped not only to climb all the chief peaks of the range, but also to map and survey the entire *massif* (block of mountains). Because of the skill and efficiency of its members, the party was able to carry out all of these objectives, and the whole expedition was crowned with success.

Halfway round the world from the rain-swept Mountains of the Moon lies a range of lower, but far more difficult peaks—the

Right: the vegetation of the Ruwenzori range, where glacier ice and luxuriant jungle crowd closely together. It is through this dense growth that expeditions have to beat a trail before reaching the base of the mountain.

Below: Walter Bonatti on the Nakitawa bridge in the Ruwenzori range. He followed the route that Abruzzi had taken. Choosing to climb solo, he was alone from the base of the glacier up to the summit of Peak Margherita.

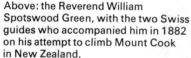

Above: the Reverend William Spotswood Green, with the two Swiss guides who accompanied him in 1882 on his attempt to climb Mount Cook in New Zealand.

so-called Southern Alps of New Zealand's South Island. The highest of these, Mount Cook, is only 12,349 feet above sea level. But its crumbling ledges, frequent avalanches, torturous glaciers, and swiftly changing weather conditions make it a challenge for the most expert mountaineer.

The first man to attempt Mount Cook was William Spotswood Green, a clergyman and member of the British Alpine Club. When, in 1882, the governor of New Zealand offered to help finance any expedition that would tackle the peaks in his country, Green was the first to answer the call. With two Swiss guides, Ulrich Kaufman and Emil Boss, he traveled to New Zealand and set off at once for Mount Cook. Even reaching the mountain was a difficult task, for the three had to make their own trail through the bush to the great Tasman Glacier at the foot of the mountain. Green and his guides, after much arduous reconnoitering, found a route up a spur of this glacier. By the second day of the climb, they had reached a snow shelf high on its upper section. The sky began to take on an ominous yellowish hue, but still they kept on, crawling over rickety rock ledges, and dodging the small ice-avalanches that swept down from above. At last they reached the final ice-wall; the summit lay not more than 200 feet ahead. But suddenly a storm sprang up. High winds swept across the precipice they clung to, lashing them with cold rain and fragments of ice. It was past 6 P.M. and already growing too dark to see. They had to turn back.

The descent was a nightmare. The rain had turned much of the surface snow and ice to slush. As they hurried down, they slipped and slid from one precarious hold to another. At last they were

enclosed in complete darkness and had to spend the night on a ledge just barely wide enough to stand on. Here they waited for dawn, cold, wet, exhausted, and without anything to eat but a few pieces of dried meat. When morning came, they made their way down to their base camp. They were glad to have escaped with their lives, but deeply disappointed that complete victory had eluded them.

It was not until Christmas Day, 1894, hat the first full ascent of Mount Cook was achieved. Appropriately enough, the men who made it—George Graham, Jack Clark, and Tom Fyfe—were New Zealanders. And it was not long before Mount Cook, Mount Tasman (11,475 feet), and others of the Southern Alps became the training ground for hundreds of young New Zealand climbers. The difficult ice, rock, and weather conditions of New Zealand's mountains have schooled many of the world's best mountaineers—among them, of course, Sir Edmund Hillary, the conqueror of Everest.

Mountain climbing began late in New Zealand. It began even later in another mountain region of the world—Antarctica. Here, in 1908, a group of explorers from Ernest Shackleton's South Polar Expedition climbed to the top of Mount Erebus (12,448 feet). In view of the inadequacy of their equipment, this first ascent of a polar peak represents a fine mountaineering achievement. In fact, although exploration of Antarctica proceeded rapidly after 1908, it was not until 1966 that the first explicitly mountaineering expedition to the region was made. Led by the American climber Nicholas Clinch, the 1966 party scaled Vinson Massif (16,864 feet) as well as a number of lesser peaks.

Mount Erebus in Antarctica was first climbed by members of Shackleton's South Polar expedition. This remarkable first ascent of a polar peak was made with practically no climbing equipment.

Scaling the North American Peaks

6

After gold was discovered in the Yukon in the year 1896, Alaska became a magnet for thousands of eager prospectors and pioneers. In 1896, one of these "sourdoughs," an American named W. A. Dickey, became the first white man to reach and explore North America's highest mountain. The local Indian tribes called it Denali, "The Great One," but Dickey, proclaiming both his political allegiance and his faith in a Republican victory, renamed it Mount McKinley, for the Republican candidate for the presidency that year. That William McKinley did, in fact, win helped make the name stick. And, thanks to the work of a survey expedition in 1897, the new president had the satisfaction of knowing that "his" mountain was higher than any other on the continent.

The first recorded sighting of Mount McKinley was in 1794, when the English navigator George Vancouver, while sailing off the Alaskan coast, noted "stupendous snow mountains" on the northern horizon. Situated a mere $3\frac{1}{2}°$ below the Arctic Circle,

McKinley and its near neighbor, Mount Foraker, rise in solitary grandeur above a bleak, flat plain. Mount McKinley, whose South Peak is 20,320 feet high, is remarkable not only for its tremendous height, but also for the almost Arctic conditions of its upper reaches. Its flanks are encrusted with manifold layers of ice, and grooved with numerous glaciers. On its upper slopes, the temperature never rises above zero, and the bitter cold is intensified by winds that sometimes exceed 100 miles per hour. These conditions make any ascent of the mountain almost a polar expedition.

The first attempt to climb the mountain took place in 1903, and was led by Judge Wickersham of the little boom town of Fairbanks, 150 miles north of McKinley. His expedition had little hope of success because none of the party possessed even a rudimentary knowledge of mountaineering technique. Instead of planning their route carefully beforehand, the party simply began climbing from the point at which they had arrived on the lower slopes. In no time

Above: the Kashawulsh Glacier in the Saint Elias range in Alaska.

Below: United States President William McKinley in 1899. The highest North American mountain was given his name. National Portrait Gallery, Smithsonian Institution, Washington, D.C.

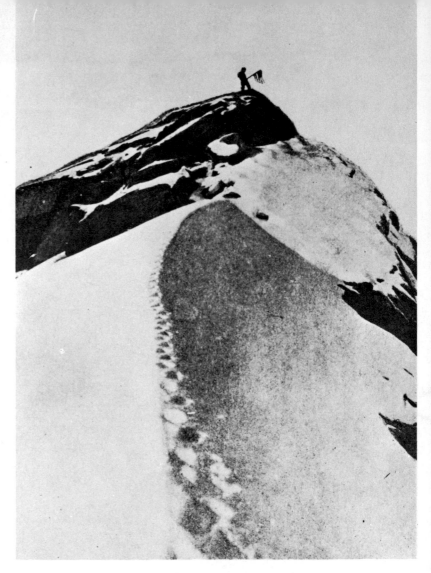

Above: Dr. Frederick Cook, wearing snow-shoes. His expedition failed to climb Mount McKinley from the south-west. He later claimed that he had conquered the mountain on a subsequent attempt.

Above right: Dr. Cook's photograph, which purported to show Burrill, his companion, on the summit. In fact, the picture was taken on a lesser peak.

at all they were defeated by walls of ice they were incapable of traversing. Giving up the attempt, Judge Wickersham went back to Fairbanks and often thereafter was heard to declare that McKinley was unclimbable.

This opinion was not shared by Dr. Frederick Cook, an explorer who had taken part in several polar expeditions in the 1890's. Dr. Cook was highly esteemed by other explorers, and it was thought that if anyone could scale the mountain he was the man. But the saga of Dr. Cook and Mount McKinley was to prove one of the oddest in the history of exploration.

In 1906, Cook, together with Herschel Parker, a physics professor, and Belmore Browne, an artist and naturalist, attempted to scale McKinley from the southwest. But after weeks of struggling to find a way through the maze of glaciers at the base of the mountain, the party was forced to abandon the climb, and return to Tyonek, the small settlement from which they had set out.

It was at this point that the venture took an unusual turn. Leaving Browne and Parker in Tyonek, Cook set off again accompanied only by Edward Barrill, one of the party's pack-carriers. What Cook told his companions was simply that he was going to explore new approaches to McKinley. Something of what he actually had in mind, however, is revealed by a telegram he sent to a friend in New York shortly before he set off: "Am preparing for a last desperate attempt on Mount McKinley."

Cook returned from his expedition within a month, announcing that he had reached McKinley's summit. To prove it, he produced slides and photographs which, he said, he had taken at the top. Over the next few years, chiefly through a book he published about his adventure, called *To the Top of the Continent,* he won considerable public acclaim. But Parker and Browne knew from the outset that Cook's triumph was a hoax. The amount of time he had been away from Tyonek was barely enough to ascend McKinley's glacier-clad lower slopes, let alone attain its summit. Cook, however, stubbornly clung to his grandiose claims until four years later, when another ascent party proved conclusively that his photographs had been taken from one of the lesser peaks near the base of McKinley.

In the meantime, Parker and Browne had not been the only ones to see through Cook's falsehood. Chief among these doubters were

A group of sourdoughs, the prospectors and trappers who lived in the country surrounding Mount McKinley, posing outside a saloon in Fairbanks. Third from the left is Billie McPhee, the bar-keeper who financed the first successful assault on the mountain. He also bet $5,000 that the expedition would reach the top before July 4, 1910.

Above: the Muldrow Glacier, used by the sourdoughs as a route to the summit.

Below: the twin peaks of Mount McKinley appear equal in height, but the South Peak, left, is 850 feet higher.

the trappers, hunters, and gold prospectors in the boom town of Alaska. Although none of them were mountaineers, they possessed a thorough knowledge of the foothills around Mount McKinley, and Cook's claim struck them as preposterous. Their response was to mount an expedition of their own.

One night, in the bitter winter of 1909, a group of "sourdoughs" —prospectors and trappers—were sitting around swapping stories in the bar-room of Billie McPhee, a saloon-keeper in Fairbanks. For the thousandth time, the talk turned to the dubious claims of Dr. Cook. Most of the men held to Judge Wickersham's opinion that the mountain would never be climbed. But two of the party, Tom Lloyd and William Taylor, disagreed. In fact, they said, they could do it themselves. Billie McPhee offered to finance the venture, and even went so far as to make a bet of $5,000 that they would reach the top before July 4, 1910.

Accordingly, on December 20, 1909, Lloyd and Taylor set out to climb Mount McKinley. With them were two hardy trappers, Peter Anderson and Charley McGonagall. None of the four had had any previous mountaineering experience and, of course, they took no

guides. They possessed no professional climbing equipment. All they carried on their two dog sleds was a quantity of rope, their usual camping gear, and sufficient food to last them several weeks. They were also armed with several intangible—and invaluable—advantages: tremendous physical fitness, indomitable pluck, and the trapper's sure instinct for pathfinding.

The men's toughness may be judged by the fact that they thought nothing of setting out in the dead of winter; their skill as pathfinders by the fact that they instinctively hit upon the one comparatively easy route up—the Muldrow Glacier. But the four reached the head of the glacier only after 11 grueling weeks of trekking. Once there, the party established their base camp. They had already climbed to 11,000 feet—much of the way in howling blizzards. Peter Anderson was suffering from a frostbitten toe but, according to the diary kept by Lloyd, he dismissed it as a mere nuisance, remarking that his foot was just "a little bit sore, as a fellow would say."

The men were able to drive their dog sleds up as far as the mountain's razor-backed saddle. There, at 15,000 feet, they discovered that McKinley had two peaks, seemingly of equal height. In fact, the South Peak is the higher of the two by about 850 feet. Unluckily, they picked the North Peak—a choice which ultimately robbed them of the technical "first" ascent of the mountain.

Their last camp before the final assault on the summit was in a hole they carved out of the ice on the steep ridge of the saddle. The next day, they started up the North Peak and kept going, cutting steps for themselves in the ice, until they reached the top. There they raised the flag of the United States on a 14-foot spruce pole which they planted firmly in the ice.

It took them only a few days to retrace their steps down to their

Left: a painting of Mount McKinley by Belmore Browne, who was a well-known artist and naturalist. His fascination with the mountain led him beyond painting the magnificent scene, to attempt the climb to the summit.

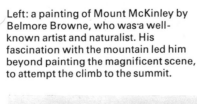

Below: Herschel Parker posing with a companion, probably Belmore Browne. They accompanied Dr. Cook on his first unsuccessful assault on Mount McKinley, and were most suspicious of his claim to have conquered the peak.

Above: Hudson Stuck, the Episcopal archdeacon of the Yukon, leader of the expedition that finally conquered the South Peak of Mount McKinley in 1913.

Above: an ice staircase chopped out of the frozen surface of Mount McKinley on the south face, to provide a way to the summit. It was methods like this which enabled the Stuck party to work their way to the top of the peak.

base camp. And in less than two weeks, Lloyd, having made excellent speed in the spring weather, was back in Fairbanks regaling his friends with the tale of their adventure.

For reasons never fully explained, Lloyd claimed that his party had scaled *both* peaks. The most plausible reason for this deception is that Lloyd, fearing that the South Peak just might prove to be the higher of McKinley's peaks, was trying to protect his friend Billie McPhee. The saloon-keeper had, after all, bet $5,000 that they would reach McKinley's *summit*. In any case, it matters little today that Lloyd and his companions scaled the lesser of the two peaks. The mastery of a mountain like McKinley by four complete amateurs remains one of mountaineering's most amazing achievements.

Sadly, few people outside Alaska credited Lloyd's account of the climb. It was not until three years later, when the party's flagstaff was seen on the North Peak by another ascent party, that the achievement of Lloyd and his companions was verified beyond a shadow of doubt.

Two years after the success of the "Sourdough Expedition," the stormy heights of Mount McKinley were the scene of a heroic failure by Herschel Parker and Belmore Browne. They planned their renewed assault on the mountain with meticulous care. Like the sourdoughs, they approached the mountain from the northeast, and were able to drive their dog sleds up to the top of the Muldrow Glacier. Leaving their dogs at the base camp, they then worked their way up the narrow ridge of the saddle. At 16,400 feet they

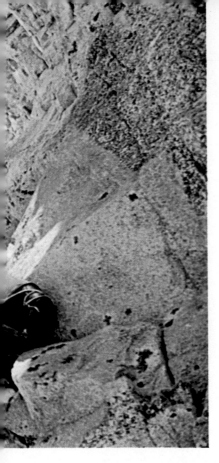

Even today, Mount McKinley is a hard climb.
Above: Zucchi, a member of Riccardo Cassin's Italian expedition, performs ice acrobatics in reaching the next step during the climb of the dangerous south face of Mount McKinley in 1961.

Above right: two members of the Italian expedition, Canali and Zucchi, stand exhausted but safe at the base camp, having returned triumphant from their climb of the "impossible wall."

pitched camp in a glacier basin and prepared to make the final long ascent. But suddenly the weather broke, and for four days they were trapped in their small tent in the midst of a savage blizzard that sent huge avalanches thundering down the mountainside.

When the weather cleared, they set off again. At 19,000 feet, with the angle of the ridge before them decreasing at each step, they felt assured of success. But a few hundred feet from the top, another terrible blizzard struck them. Painfully, they struggled on, but a mere 300 feet below the summit the two men reached the limits of their endurance and had to turn back. They reached their camp only after many arduous hours. Two days afterward, the weather again cleared and they made one last attempt, but again they were driven back by a sudden storm when they were only a short distance from the top.

But if Parker and Browne had been unlucky in one regard, they were miraculously lucky in another. In the late summer of 1912, only a matter of days after they had left McKinley, the entire mountain was shaken by a series of earthquakes. Vast portions of McKinley's slopes were sheered off in a succession of avalanches, and the very crest of the final ridge they had stood on collapsed and fell away. Thus in 1913, when the South Peak was scaled for the first time, McKinley was in a sense a different mountain.

The 1913 ascent was led by Hudson Stuck, the Episcopal archdeacon of the Yukon territory. An experienced mountaineer, he had climbed often in the Rocky Mountains since his arrival in the

Above: an aerial photograph of the sea of snow-capped peaks extending for miles in the incredible expanse of the mountain ranges of Alaska.

United States as an Englishman of 22. When he set out, at the age of 50, to conquer North America's highest peak, he was fulfilling an ambition he had cherished for many years.

Stuck's party included a young missionary named Robert Tatum, a native Alaskan named Walter Harper, and a prospector named Harry P. Karstens. Like the expeditions that had preceded them, Stuck and his party made their way up the Muldrow Glacier and prepared to follow on up the northern ridge that had been described to them. But it was a ridge no longer. The cataclysm of the previous year had so shattered and disrupted the contours of the mountain that the ridge had become a jagged ice-wall of spurs and pinnacles. All the way up this wall, they methodically cut a massive ice stair-case, climbing up and down its thousands of steps many times to bring up supplies.

Stuck's party made their final assault on the South Peak on June 6, 1913. At the top, Stuck gave thanks to God for their success. This done, in venerable Alpine tradition he set about taking baro-meter and thermometer readings. He left one of the thermometers on the mountain to be checked by later expeditions. When it was recovered 19 years later, its indicator had fallen well below the bottom of the scale, the lowest reading of which was $-95\,°$F.

In the spring of 1932, Mount McKinley was the object of two expeditions. The first of these, led by Erling Strom and Harry J. Liek was interesting for its extensive use of skis on the ascent of the lower slopes, and for its achievement of the first conquest of *both* peaks. The second, led by the brilliant young climber Allan Carpé, was notable for its highly scientific nature: the study of cosmic rays in higher altitudes.

Carpé's party made use of an airplane to land supplies—the first time such a thing had been attempted on a glacier. This operation was watched by the Strom-Liek party as they climbed high above the glacier on Karstens Ridge. On their descent, they hoped to meet up with Carpé and his colleague Theodore Koven, to compare notes about the climb. But when they reached Carpé's camp, they found the tents deserted. The victims of some inexplicable accident, both men had fallen to their deaths a mile and a half down the mountain.

McKinley was climbed comparatively rarely until shortly after World War II, when the famed Alaskan mountaineer Bradford Washburn proposed several new routes to the summit based on aerial photographs of the mountain. To test these routes, a number of expeditions were launched, and one of them, led by the Italian climber Riccardo Cassin in 1961, achieved the remarkable feat of scaling McKinley's sheer south face—until then known as the "impossible wall."

The Alaska Range, to which McKinley and its neighbor Foraker belong, is but one of numerous ranges in the great mountain system that stretches from Alaska to the tip of South America, taking in the Canadian and American Rockies, the Cascade range, the Sierra Nevada, the Mexican mountains, and the Andes.

One of the most interesting of the northern ranges in this system is the Saint Elias, a chain of volcanic mountains which straddles the border between Alaska and the Yukon Territory. Among

Below: Andy Taylor's dog team. Taylor was the sourdough guide who accompanied Captain MacCarthy on his first ascent of Mount Logan. The dogs took supplies to the base camp.

ARCTIC OCEAN

ASIA

GREENL.

ARCTIC CIRCLE

PARRY ISLANDS

BANKS I.

VICTORIA I.

BROOKS RANGE

BAFFIN ISLAND

Yukon

MT. McKINLEY
20,320

Alaska

Fairbanks

MT. FORAKER
17,395

Great
Bear L.

ALEUTIAN IS.

MT. LUCANIA
MT. BONA
MT. ST. ELIAS MT. LOGAN
18,008   19,850

MACKENZIE RA.

Mackenzie

Gt. Slave
Lake

HUDSON

Ungava
Pena.

L.
Athabasca

BAY

QUEEN
CHARLOTTE
ISLANDS

COAST MOUNTAINS

Fraser

MT. ROBSON
12,972

Edmonton

Saskatchewan

Lake
Winnipeg

Nelson

Laurentian Shield

VANCOUVER I.

Vancouver

MT. ASSINIBOINE
11,870

S. Saskatchewan

Albany

Lake
Superior

OTTA
M

MT. OLYMPUS
7954

CASCADE RA.

MT. RAINIER
14,410

Blue Mts.

Columbia

Snake

BITTERROOT RA.

Missouri

Lake
Michigan

Huron

Lake
Ontario

L. Erie

Mo

C. Medocino

MT. SHASTA
14,162

Great Salt

Gt.
Salt L.

ABSAROKA

DEVIL'S
TOWER
517

BIG
HORN
MTS.

BLACK
HILLS

Chicago

APPALACH.

Yosemite Nat'l Park

San Francisco

SIERRA NEVADA

Basin

Wasatch

LONGS PK.
14,256

Platte

Missouri

MT. WHITNEY
14,495

Death
Valley

Grand Canyon

Colorado

SHIPROCK
7178

MT. ELBERT
14,431

ROCKY MOUNTAINS

Ozark Plateau

BOSTON
MTS.

Ohio

MT. MITCH.
6584

Gila

Arkansas

OUACHITA
MTS.

Mississippi

PACIFIC

TROPIC OF CANCER

Lower California

Rio Grande

SACRAMENTO MTS.

Red

New Orleans

Flor

20°

140°

C. Falso

SA. MADRE OCCIDENTAL

SA. MADRE ORIENTAL

Rio Grande

GULF OF MEXICO

OCEAN

Mexico City

Yucatan

C

POPOCATÉPETL
17,887

16,701
ORIZABA

60°   180°   160°   140°   120°   100°   80°   60°   40°

180°

160°

40°

0   200   400   600   800   1000
Miles

120°

100°

86

Left: the North American mountain system stretches from Alaska south through the Canadian and American Rockies, the Mexican mountains, and finally links up with the Andes of South America.

Above: the years between the wars saw the majority of North American peaks conquered. One of the leading climbers of this period was Bradford Washburn, standing second from the right here in the Mount Marcus Baker expedition.

the highest peaks in this chain is Mount Saint Elias (18,008 feet). This peak holds a special place in climbing history, for it was with its first ascent, by the Duke of the Abruzzi in 1897, that North American mountaineering really began.

The Duke, a grandson of King Victor Emmanuel II of Italy, was only 24 when he led the ascent of Mount Saint Elias. Nevertheless, wrote Count Aldo Bonacossa, "he was already a leader of men [and although] he was sometimes a little exacting in his demands . . . how striking was his personal example in endurance and in dangers." The Italian expedition he headed included the famous mountain photographer Vittorio Sella, as well as a number of noted Alpine guides and mountaineers. It took the party nearly a month to reach the summit, and the expedition, which carried out a great deal of exploration, took 154 days in all.

The Duke's conquest of Mount Saint Elias provoked a sudden upsurge of interest in climbing in North America, and the three decades that followed saw many brilliant achievements in Alaska, Canada, and the United States. European as well as American mountaineers played an important part in the pioneering climbs of this era. Edward Whymper, for example, spent four years in western Canada at the beginning of the century, and did much to popularize this new area.

By the mid-1920's, most of the major peaks in Canada had been climbed, including Mount Robson, the highest in the Canadian Rockies. Just 12,972 feet high, Robson is not one of the world's highest peaks, but it is certainly one of the most impressive, towering in lordly splendor above the many lesser peaks of the region. First climbed in 1913, it has not often been attempted since then because of the constant danger of avalanches in its upper reaches.

Left: El Capitan and the Merced River in Yosemite Valley, California, the rock climbers' most challenging area. Many of the techniques developed here have had a great influence on methods of international mountaineering.

Right: the tiny figure of a climber can be seen edging his way up the west face of the Leaning Tower, one of the many vast granite outcrops in Yosemite.

Robson's 1913 conqueror was Captain A. H. MacCarthy, one of Canada's most distinguished climbers. MacCarthy had many notable "firsts" to his credit when, in 1925, he led the heroic first assault on Mount Logan (19,850 feet). This mountain, the second highest in North America, is situated in the Saint Elias range, and, like many of the peaks in the region, is almost inaccessible. Before he could begin to plan the ascent, MacCarthy had to spend considerable time locating a route to the lower slopes of the mountain. The next step was to prepare the way for the expedition proper. In the dead of winter, MacCarthy and his sourdough guide, Andy Taylor, pioneered a route up the mountain's outlying glaciers and set up a chain of camps and supply depots for use during the forthcoming assault.

In late May, 1925, the nine members of MacCarthy's assault team at last set off for Mount Logan. The expedition included no porters, and each climber had to carry a 70 pound load of supplies. Their route was almost entirely over snow and ice, and for 44 days, as they fought their way steadily upward, the men were assailed by almost continual blizzards. Visibility was frequently reduced to a mere yard or two, and the high winds piled up drifts of loose snow in which they frequently sank up to their chests.

The party made its last camp at 18,500 feet. The final 1,350 feet to the top took them almost the whole of the next day, and when, at 8 P.M., they stood at last on Canada's highest peak, they had little time for jubilation. Ahead lay the descent, which was to prove a great deal more dangerous than the grueling climb. Within minutes of their setting out on the return journey, another savage blizzard closed in around them. From then on, the trek back to their base camp was one long nightmare of driving snow and freezing ice. At one point they lost their way and discovered to their horror that they were retracing their steps back to the summit. Only after three terrible days—two nights of which they spent in the open—did they reach the safety of their camp. Truly, as the mountaineering historian Arnold Lunn has said of MacCarthy's party, "For endurance and courage, their achievement has rarely been surpassed."

Between the two world wars, North American mountaineering really came of age. One of the foremost mountaineers of this period

was Bradford Washburn, who headed an impressive number of Alaskan expeditions. Many of these had the dual purpose of exploration and scientific investigation. Chief among Washburn's achievements was his ascent of Canada's second highest peak, Mount Lucania (17,150 feet) in the Saint Elias Range in 1937.

Outside Alaska, the highest mountain in the United States is Mount Whitney (14,495 feet), named for the geologist J. Dwight Whitney. Located in the southern Sierra Nevada of California, this lofty peak provides a dramatic contrast to nearby Death Valley, which, at 282 feet below sea level, is the lowest point in the country.

It is somewhat ironic that the United States, with one of the world's most extensive mountain systems, has very few peaks to challenge the mountaineer. The Rocky Mountains, the Cascade range, and the Sierra Nevada cover thousands of square miles, contain many peaks of 13,000 feet and more, yet they can offer nothing to equal the arduous and testing ascents of the Alps. With very few exceptions, these sprawling ranges possess easy contours and gentle gradients, and, although difficult routes can be sought out, the majority of the highest points can be reached with only a stiff uphill walk.

One of the favorite centers for amateur climbers in the United States is Mount Rainier (14,410 feet) in the Cascade Range in Washington state. An extinct volcano, the mountain is snow-capped and covered with no less than 26 glaciers.

But outside Alaska, the most demanding climbs are not on mountains at all, but on the towering rock formations of the American Southwest. Yosemite National Park in central California, for example, offers over 300 rock-climbing routes, of which two-thirds rank among the four highest grades of difficulty. Some of the most exacting of these are the three Cathedral Rocks, the northwest face of the Half Dome, and the Salathé Wall of El Capitan. The difficulties confronting climbers in the Yosemite Valley may be appreciated in terms of the fact that a rock climb here may take anything from 3 to 10 days. In recent years, ever more dangerous climbs have been attempted and achieved in Yosemite.

Another difficult rock climb is offered by Shiprock Butte (1,678 feet), a sheer volcanic outcrop rising out of the New Mexican plateau. Still another is provided by the famous Devils Tower of northeastern Wyoming. Rising perpendicularly 865 feet above the surrounding hills like a prehistoric skyscraper, it was long thought to be unclimbable. However, since it was first scaled in 1937, it has become one of the classic rock climbs of America; during one week in 1956 it was climbed no fewer than 81 times.

Thus, while North America has few mountains to equal the challenges of the Alps, the Andes, or the Himalaya, its Alaskan peaks and its rock pinnacles offer superb training opportunities for the climber. Having served their apprenticeships on their home ground, American mountaineers have gone out to conquer some of the world's greatest peaks.

Meeting the South American Challenge

7

One of the most remarkable incidents in the history of mountaineering occurred in 1521, when a handful of Spanish soldiers climbed to the top of Popocatépetl in central Mexico. Popocatépetl ("The Smoking Mountain") is an inactive volcano. Although its sloping sides do not present serious climbing difficulties, its height alone—17,887 feet—is enough to discourage all but the most strongly-motivated climbers. But we may be sure that the soldiers who made the ascent in 1521 were strongly motivated, for they were acting under the strict orders of their commander, Hernando Cortes. Under the fierce leadership of this man, the Spanish had brought the mighty Aztec empire to its knees. But the Spaniards' continued power in Mexico depended on their superior weaponry, and they were now desperately short of the sulfur they needed to make gunpowder. It was for the purpose of obtaining this vital mineral that Cortes ordered his men to climb Popocatépetl. If they could reach its summit, they could get sulfur from its crater.

Left: a Mexican family standing at the foot of Popocatépetl. Although nearly 18,000 feet high, the gentle slopes of the volcano present no real challenge to an experienced climber.

Above: Spanish soldiers under Cortes made the first ascent of Popocatépetl in 1521, to collect sulfur from the crater for gunpowder. This mural of the guns in action is by Diego Rivera.

91

Above: volcanoes have fascinated men since Von Humboldt. Here a climber is seen on Ecuador's Mount Sangay.

Below: Indians of the high Andes have become physically adapted to their life at high altitudes over the centuries.

Cortes' soldiers did not disappoint him. They reached the top and returned to camp laden with quantities of sulfur. No doubt Cortes congratulated himself on having solved his ammunition supply problem in so novel a manner. He little knew that, in carrying out his orders, his soldiers had climbed higher than anyone had ever done before, and had set a height record that remained unbroken for centuries.

Popocatépetl, which today is the dominant feature on the horizon of Mexico City, is but one of many volcanic peaks in the Volcanic Axis, a chain of mountains stretching across Mexico in the south. This mountain chain contains some of the most beautiful peaks in the Americas. Orizaba, for example, which, at 18,701 feet is the third highest mountain in North America, possesses the almost perfect symmetry of Mount Fuji. Unlike Fuji, however, Orizaba and the other volcanic peaks of the Volcanic Axis rise above tropical forest. In fact, the contrast between the cool serenity of their snow-capped summits and the teeming life of the jungle at their feet is one of the most characteristic features of the Mexican mountains. Just as typical, however, is the lack of challenge they offer the experienced mountaineer. Again, Orizaba is a good

example. Despite its height, it affords a remarkably easy ascent. Most of the way up to its snow-line can be accomplished on horse-back!

There could be no more dramatic contrast to the gentle slopes of the Mexican mountains than the sheer drops and rugged heights of the Andes. Extending some 4,500 miles down the western coast of South America—all the way from Panama to Cape Horn—the Andes have been called the longest unbroken mountain system in the world. Throughout this great series of mountain ranges, there are lofty and forbidding peaks which have challenged, and continue to challenge, the nerve and endurance of the world's most experienced mountaineers.

The exploration of the Andes began in the early 1700's with a French and Spanish expedition to the mountains of Ecuador. Here, just south of the Equator, the expedition leaders, Bouguer and La Condamine, carried out the first scientific exploration of high altitudes.

The Ecuadorian mountains—most of which are of volcanic origin —were again the subject of investigation in 1802. In that year, Alexander von Humboldt, a German scientist and geographer, went to Ecuador to climb and study two volcanic peaks: Cotopaxi (19,344 feet) and Chimborazo (20,577 feet). In neither case did he succeed in gaining the summit, although he did reach a height of over 19,000 feet on Chimborazo.

Seventy years after Von Humboldt's visit to Ecuador, another German scientist, Wilhelm Reiss, and his companion, A. M. Escobar, made the first complete ascent of Cotopaxi. This mountain is the

Right: Alexander von Humboldt, a German scientist and geographer, in his library. He climbed nearly to the summit of two volcanoes in Ecuador, Cotopaxi and Chimborazo, during his scientific researches in South America

highest live volcano in the world. Nevertheless, in common with many other volcanic peaks, the slopes leading up to its snow-covered cone slant very gently, at an angle of about 30°.

Chimborazo, the second mountain that Von Humboldt had attempted in 1802, was not fully scaled until 1880. In that year Edward Whymper, then aged 40, in company with his one-time rival Jean-Antoine Carrel, journeyed to South America in search of peaks as yet unclimbed. Having laid to rest the bitter antagonisms of their youth, the two mountaineers made an excellent climbing

Below: a party of English climbers on Popocatépetl in about 1900. They are masked against sunburn. Other common hazards of high altitude climbing are extreme cold, high winds, and oxygen starvation, which causes mountain sickness.

team. Together they made short work of Cotopaxi (theirs was the fifth ascent of the mountain) and scaled several lesser virgin peaks. They then addressed themselves to Chimborazo. Unlike Cotopaxi, this is an inactive volcano, and its flanks are grooved with glaciers which greatly increase the difficulties of the ascent. Whymper and Carrel, however, reached Chimborazo's summit on their first attempt, and, in doing so, far surpassed any of their previous height records.

For 25 years after Whymper and Carrel's ascent, Chimborazo remained the highest mountain ever climbed in South America. Interestingly enough, it had once been erroneously considered the highest mountain on earth as a result of Bouguer and La Condamine's investigations in the 1700's. But "The Watch Tower of the World," as the South American liberator Simón Bolívar called Chimborazo, is not even the highest mountain in South America. That honor is held by Aconcagua, which towers 22,834 feet high in Argentina near the Chile border.

The loftiest peak in the whole of the Western Hemisphere, Aconcagua presents the climber with three deadly hazards: loose rocks, high, bitterly cold winds, and thin air. Because of the howling gales which continually buffet Aconcagua, there is relatively little snow and ice for the climber to contend with. But if the wind sweeps away the snow, it also loosens the rock face, making each foot and hand hold treacherous. Moreover, the icy gusts make it doubly difficult to breathe in the thin air of the heights. For every breath he draws, the climber must struggle against an unseen but powerful enemy—the bitterly cold wind that seems to suck the very oxygen from the air.

The first expedition to be successful in overcoming these hazards was led by the British alpinist, Edward FitzGerald, in 1896-1897. Two years before, he and the famous Swiss guide Mattias Zurbriggen had made the first ascents of Mount Tasman and Mount Sefton in New Zealand. Zurbriggen was again FitzGerald's guide on this expedition. Also in the party was a young English climber named Stuart Vines and an Italian guide named Nicolo Lanti. In addition to these four, the expedition also included a number of other climbers and a host of porters.

The first problem facing the expedition was to locate the base of the mountain itself, for although Aconcagua's upper slopes rise in magnificent isolation from its surrounding foothills, its lower

Above: the hardships of an Andes ascent are often matched by the difficulties of reaching the base of the mountain. Here a climber with a machete cuts down dense growth to reach Mount Sangay.

approaches are obscured by them. After weeks of frustrating detours and minor mishaps, FitzGerald and his party reached their objective —a point 14,000 feet above sea level on Aconcagua's Horcones Glacier. It was nearly Christmas Day—midsummer in the Southern Hemisphere—when the party pitched its first camp on Aconcagua. Above them towered nearly 9,000 feet of windswept snow and crumbling rock, and already a large number of the men who had set out with the expedition had dropped out. Only a few of the porters remained with FitzGerald, Zurbriggen, Vines, and Lanti when, on January 14, 1897, they began the assault.

As they slowly worked their way up the loose shale of the mountainside, the men began to suffer from severe bouts of mountain sickness. Essentially oxygen starvation, this condition can strike the climber at any height over 7,000 feet. It results from there being an inadequate supply of oxygen to the blood and body tissues, and is characterized by weakness, nausea, shortness of breath, and the

Left: as elsewhere in the world, the South American climber finds the local people of invaluable help as guides and porters to help him transport his essential equipment to the mountain. On this expedition to climb Mount Sangay everything had to be carried through forests, prickly grass—as shown here—and even over an area of lava which was still hot enough to burn through the rubber soles of the climbers' shoes.

Below: FitzGerald, leader of the 1896-1897 expedition to Aconcagua, the highest peak in South America.

kind of depression that robs a man of his will-power and concentration. Given a few days, the body can adapt or "acclimatize" itself fairly well to rarified air conditions at heights between 7,000 and 18,000 feet. But at heights of over 18,000 feet, even prolonged rest-stops cannot ensure that a man will not be suddenly and totally incapacitated by an attack of mountain sickness.

Aconcagua's particularly rarified air made FitzGerald's party highly susceptible to the effects of high altitude—and they had now passed the 18,000 foot mark. Nevertheless, though they were trembling with sickness and exhaustion, and chilled to the very marrow by the winds that howled around them, they pressed forward. Sometimes it took several hours to progress a few feet over the precarious scree of the mountainside, and four times they were forced to retreat to a camp lower down to recover their energies. Then the weather cleared slightly, and, on their fifth attempt, they managed to reach a point less than 1,000 feet from the summit with relative ease. Here, with success seemingly near at hand, they rested and took some food. This proved a disastrous mistake. Once again, FitzGerald, who had been weak throughout the climb, was racked by sickness. There was nothing to be done but to help him back to the last camp. Vines and Lanti undertook this task, leaving Zurbriggen to attempt a solo attack on the mountain top. Once more the Swiss guide set his face to the summit. This time, after several hours of doggedly inching his way forward, he planted his ice-ax on Aconcagua's highest point.

A week afterward, Zurbriggen's success was repeated by Vines and Lanti. FitzGerald, however, remained too ill to attempt the final assault again. It is one of the ironies of mountaineering history that the man who planned and led the first conquest of the Americas' highest peak was denied the satisfaction of experiencing that conquest himself.

Soon after their ascent of Aconcagua, FitzGerald's party made their way to another lofty peak on the Argentina-Chile border.

Right: Lord Conway of Allington, the famous British climber who climbed Aconcagua a year after FitzGerald, and then went on to lead the first assault on Mount Illimani in Bolivia. Conway was a truly international climber who explored mountains the world over.

Far right: a photograph taken by Conway in 1898 of the Harvard Observatory Meteorological Station on the summit of El Misti, the extinct volcano which was important to the ancient Inca civilisation.

Below: Mount Aconcagua towers 22,834 feet above sea level. The altitude and the regular buffeting from icy winds make it one of South America's most difficult peaks to scale. The members of FitzGerald's expedition suffered from the weather, nearly having to give up the assault.

This was Tupungato, 22,310 feet high. FitzGerald himself did not take part in the ascent. Again the final assault was by Mattias Zurbriggen—this time with Stuart Vines, In fact, on this occasion the Swiss guide did not actually lead the way to the summit. As the two men hauled themselves onto the ridge leading to the point that had appeared to be the summit, they were startled to discover that the mountain possessed a still higher peak about an hour's climb away. Overcome by exhaustion and possibly by the depression that so often assails men at high altitudes, Zurbriggen was prepared to give up and go back down. Stuart Vines, however, was not. Picking up his ice-ax, he pushed on again, not stopping until he stood on Tupungato's true summit. Not to be outdone, Zurbriggen then mustered his remaining strength, and followed Vines to the top.

The year after FitzGerald's expedition, another British party arrived in the Andes. This group, led by the explorer-mountaineer Martin Conway, (later Lord Conway), repeated the success of FitzGerald's party by climbing Aconcagua. Conway's team then proceeded to Illimani, the twin-peaked mountain which broods over La Paz, capital of Bolivia. Illimani is one of the highest of the mountains in the Cordillera Real section of the Bolivian Andes. Conway chose to scale the lesser of its two summits. Even so, at 21,151 feet, the peak offered its first climbers an impressive challenge. Nor was it only the mountain that taxed their fortitude and resourcefulness. The native Bolivians, who had been hired to carry their goods and equipment, proved to be both frightened and uncooperative. Conway said later that they were slower than any porters he had ever before encountered. And, when he and the rest of the party reached the ice ridges on the higher slopes of Illimani, the porters flatly refused to go a step farther—even to win the silver coins that until then had served to persuade them over the difficult stretches. This

Left: South America showing the Andes, the world's longest mountain chain. This great range stretches some 4,500 miles down the entire west coast of the continent from Panama to Cape Horn.

"strike" on the part of the men who carried the party's vital supplies might have put an end to the ascent had it not been for Conway's two guides, Antoine Naquiznaz and Louis Pellisier. For the remainder of the climb, these two men generously undertook the duties of the porters, and in so doing made it possible for the expedition to reach Illimani's summit.

Northwest of Illimani, in the Cordillera Blanca region in west-central Peru, stands a mountain called Huascarán. At 22,205 feet, it is the loftiest peak in Peru and is one of the few major peaks in the world first scaled by a woman. Her name was Miss Annie Peck, and the story of her conquest of Huascarán—as she herself recorded it in her book *A Search for the Apex of America*—is a dramatic one. Annie Peck was a school teacher from Providence, Rhode Island. At the age of 45 she traveled to Europe and climbed the Matterhorn. From that moment on, she was passionately addicted to mountaineering. She spent her summer vacations climbing, and within a few years had to her credit an impressive number of ascents—including an assault on Bolivia's 21,490 foot high Mount Illampu (Sorata).

She was a small but exceptionally hardy woman, and possessed a courage and determination that put many of her male colleagues to shame. In 1908, at the age of 58, Miss Peck set her heart on conquering Huascarán. At that time its exact height was not known, but she was convinced, from an earlier reconnaissance of the mountain, that it was at least 24,000 feet high. If that were true, Huascarán's conquerer could claim the first ascent of the highest mountain in the Western Hemisphere. (Aconcagua, whose height was then known, is less than 23,000 feet high).

Huascarán possesses twin peaks. Leading up to the saddle between the two is an enormous glacier, deeply crevassed. The inherent difficulties of the approach—which Annie Peck had decided should be up the glacier—demanded experienced Alpine guides. Accordingly, she enlisted the aid of two Swiss mountaineers, Gabriel and Rudolf Taugwalder, who joined her in New York and traveled with her to Peru.

The initial stages of the climb went well. But at 11,000 feet, Rudolf Taugwalder was suddenly overcome by a debilitating attack of mountain sickness. Too ill to go on with the ascent, he had to return down the mountain with some of the party's Peruvian porters.

Above: Miss Annie Peck, an American schoolteacher who, at 45, began to climb mountains, and became one of the few women to conquer a major unclimbed peak, Mount Huascarán.

Annie Peck and Gabriel Taugwalder, however, continued on over a treacherous surface of sheer ice, powdery snow, and yawning crevasses. Twice they made camp on the steep slope of the glacier. On the third day, they found themselves inching their way up the 80° angle of the final ice-wall to the saddle. It was hard going, for they had to cut steps in the ice to serve as footholds all the way up. On the fourth day, they reached the saddle, a tilted expanse of glittering snow 20,000 feet above sea level. At either end stood a towering peak. Annie Peck chose to make for the northern pinnacle, because it seemed to offer the better ascent route. She could only hope and pray that it was the higher of the two peaks.

Miss Peck and her guide started for the peak at dawn on the morning of the fifth day. A bitterly cold wind began assailing them and Gabriel, who was doing all the cutting of the ice-steps in the towering wall they clung to, was soon trembling with exhaustion. Worse still, he began to show signs of mountain sickness. Ahead of them still lay many hundreds of feet of ice-wall. Behind lay a precipitous staircase of ice. Miss Peck and Taugwalder knew that the descent down that staircase would require all the nerve and strength they could muster. With Gabriel ill, it would be utter recklessness to continue going forward. Reluctantly, they turned their backs on the summit and retraced their steps.

Diminishing food supplies and the continued illness of her guides prevented Annie Peck from making another attempt right away. But she was far from giving up. Ten days after she had left Huascarán, she was back with fresh supplies to try again. And the Taugwalders, by now fully recovered, were as determined as she to succeed.

More familiar with their adversary on this second attempt, the three made rapid progress up the lower part of the mountain. In fact, they reached the ice-wall above the glacier in half the time it had taken them on the first ascent. They proceeded up this precipice at a steady pace and gained the saddle. Here they made their third camp. The following day, in the light of early dawn, they began the final assault on the north peak. The weather was fair, but bitterly cold. They were operating in sub-zero temperatures dressed only in layers of wool—the anorak and other protective gear worn by modern climbers had not yet become standard equipment.

As the three toiled up the glittering spine of the north peak, it seemed that they would be overcome by exhaustion and the numbing cold before they could reach the top. But the way ahead gradually became less steep, and suddenly the summit lay only a few yards away. Staggering toward it, Annie Peck became aware that she had lost the feeling in her left hand. She snatched off her mitten and saw that her fingers had turned unnaturally white. Frostbite! Another few minutes and the tissues would be completely frozen. As she

The Peruvian Andes, seen from the air, stretch away into the distance as an impersonal expanse of indomitable and silent fortresses of snow and ice.

dragged herself forward, she beat her hand against her leg over and over again, and slowly the beginnings of feeling returned to her numbed fingers.

When at last their feet touched the summit, the three climbers were almost too worn out to enjoy their triumph. Before them lay a terrifying descent down the steep ice-staircase to their last camp on the snow-covered saddle. Night had fallen and the remaining food they carried had frozen solid. Shaking with exhaustion, one after the other slipped and almost fell. Most terrible of all, Rudolf

Left: climbers at the base of Mount Yerupajá. The mountain, not one of the world's highest, qualifies as one of the most terrifying to climb. Its summit, an ice ridge with sheer sides, is like the blade of a giant knife.

Taugwalder lost both his gloves, and had to make much of the final descent barehanded. When they finally reached camp, he tried desperately to bring back the feeling in his hands by rubbing them with snow, but it was too late—all of one hand and the fingers of the other later had to be amputated.

On the summit of Huascarán's north peak, Miss Peck had been unable to carry out the tests necessary to determine its height, but she was convinced that it was at least 24,000 feet high. Unfortunately, one year later, a French survey proved it to be no more than 22,205 feet, and even then, the south peak was higher than the one she had climbed. Moreover, in later decades, many mountaineers have been inclined to doubt that she and the Taugwalders actually succeeded in reaching the very top of the north peak. But however that may be, we do know that she made a very gallant attempt on this Andean giant, and deserves the name "The Lady of Huascarán."

Many of the other mountains of Peru have been the subject of daring and eventful climbs. One of these, made by the Americans Dave Harrah and G. Maxwell in 1950, was the first ascent of Yerupajá (21,758 feet). This mountain, although not one of the world's highest, is one of its most terrible. It is often referred to as "The Butcher," because its summit consists, not of a single high point, but of a long, knife-edge ridge, like that of a butcher's cleaver. Almost perpendicular walls of ice fall away from this terrifying knife-edge *arête* (ridge) on both sides.

Above: an expedition member edges precariously up one of the sharply sloping ice ridges guarding the summit of Mount Yerupajá. The climb was successful, although the descending climbers had to spend an icy night clinging to frozen rock.

In many ways, Harrah and Maxwell's experience on Yerupajá was similar to that of Annie Peck and the Taugwalders on Huascarán. After an ascent that had called forth every ounce of their reserves, they found themselves still on the face at nightfall, and had to spend 12 hours clinging to the icy wall in the intense cold before they could get back to their last campsite. Both men suffered frostbite and Harrah later had to have all his toes amputated. It is a measure of the severe conditions in the Andes that frostbite is almost as constant a danger there as it is in the Himalaya.

The Peruvian Andes occupy an important place in history, for it was in these rugged and inaccessible highlands that the ancient civilizations of South America arose and flourished. The last of these great Indian civilizations was that of the Inca, who built their cities and temples in the mountains of Peru, Ecuador, and Chile. It was to these lofty strongholds that the last stubborn Inca people fled when the gold-hungry Spanish conquistadors swept through the Inca empire in the 1500's.

Perhaps the most famous of the final Inca mountain dwelling places is Machu Picchu, discovered by the American scholar-explorer Hiram Bingham in 1912. First and foremost an archeologist, Bingham was also an enthusiastic amateur mountaineer. In 1911, he scaled the awe-inspiring peak of Coropuna (21,700 feet) in Peru. Three years later he led a party to the summit of Salcantay (20,550 feet), which stands near the ancient Inca capital of Cusco in the Cordillera de Vilcanota of southern Peru.

The expeditions Bingham led in search of Inca ruins were sponsored by Yale University. Another university, Harvard, later established an astronomical observatory on Peru's El Misti (19,098 feet), an extinct volcano which once occupied an important place of honor in the Inca religion.

The Andes today are the site of increasing numbers of climbing expeditions by mountaineers from all over the world. One of the most unusual of these expeditions took place in mid-1970, when a team of British climbers attempted to scale the 19,400 foot El Toro in Peru. The highest remaining unscaled peak in all of South America, El Toro is unique among all the world's mountains in being the site of accidentally buried treasure. In 1954, an aircraft carrying 29 people and almost $100,000 worth of gold bullion crashed on its summit. The fate of its passengers was sealed by the impossibility

Machu Picchu, the magnificent fortress-city built by the Incas high in the Peruvian Andes. It was here that many Incas sought refuge as their empire was ravaged by the ruthless Spaniards. Machu Picchu was rediscovered when, in 1912, Hiram Bingham, an American scholar-explorer, stumbled on the site.

of mounting an adequate rescue team in time. But what of its cargo of gold? The 1970 British climbing team hoped to be able to ascertain, in the course of their attempt on the peak, whether it would be possible to recover the bullion.

Unfortunately, a mere 150 feet from El Toro's summit, the expedition was forced to abandon the climb because of the treacherous overhanging cornices of ice on the ridge and the condition of the snow, which was extremely powdery and waist-deep in places. They did discover the fate of the lost bullion, however. They found evidence to indicate that the plane had fallen from the mountainside into the glacier below. There the aircraft and its treasure must remain until the glacier eventually empties itself out, in the foothills of the mountain, hundreds of years from now.

Exploring the Himalaya

8

Nowhere in the world is there another mountain system to compare with the Himalaya. Hundreds of its peaks are similar in height to the loftiest mountains of the Andes or the Pamirs, and scores more are higher again by several thousand feet. The Himalaya are colossal in extent as well as in height. Forming the southern part of the massive central Asian highlands, the successive ranges of the Himalaya stretch the entire length of northern India, and cover most of Nepal, Sikkim, Bhutan, and southern Tibet as well.

Mountain passes through the great walls of peaks and ridges surrounding the Himlayan kingdoms are few and far between, and are rarely less than 15,000 feet high. Moreover, the storms and avalanches that accompany the yearly monsoons make even the existing passes inaccessible except during a few short months of the year. Consequently, although there has always been some trade among the peoples of the Himalaya, the little communities of farmers and herdsmen in the highlands have generally been as cut

Left: one of the fascinations of the Himalayan area is its inaccessibility. There are few routes through the vast mountain chain, and the passes which exist are seldom below 15,000 feet. Outsiders making their way into the isolated villages locked in the high valleys have found the simplicity and warm good humor of the Himalayan people particularly attractive. This 1826 drawing, by James Manson, a British survey officer, shows a Nepalese herdsman with his goats.

Right: the first Europeans to travel in the Himalayan kingdoms were the Jesuits. This painting of the early 1600's shows a prince receiving two of the Portuguese Jesuit missionaries

off from one another as their countries have been from the outside world.

Common to all the peoples of the Himalaya is a deep respect and reverence for the peaks that tower above them. Serene, majestic, and utterly remote from all earthly concerns, these lofty turrets of snow and ice have been held sacred in the highland countries for thousands of years. Many of the individual peaks are accorded special honor as being the homes of gods or goddesses. The very word "Himalaya" comes from an ancient Sanskrit phrase meaning "House of Snow." But it is not only the Himalayan peoples in whom the mountains arouse a feeling of reverence and humility. No mountaineer has traveled to this land of silent, snow-clad peaks without being deeply affected by their almost ethereal purity and massive simplicity.

The first Europeans to enter this awesome terrain and reach the mysterious and romantic kingdoms beyond India were Jesuit missionaries. Indomitable in their crusade to win converts to the faith, they had begun traveling to places as far away as Japan in the early 1500's. In 1624, two Portuguese Jesuits, Father Antonio de Andrade and Brother Manuel Marques, set out from northern India. After a journey of four months, they reached Ladakh in north-western Kashmir, where they established a church. The church was kept going for several decades by a succession of courageous Jesuit fathers who crossed and recrossed the western Himalaya in the service of the faith. In the meantime, Jesuit missionaries were also venturing into the eastern ranges of the Himalaya, and in 1714, one of them, Father Ippolito Desideri, traveled as far north as Lhasa, the sacred city of Tibet.

But the Jesuits were not map-makers, and despite the missionaries' travels, men still knew almost nothing about the size and scope of the mighty Himalayan ranges, their chief peaks, or the maze of valleys, gorges, foothills, and ridges that guarded them. Real exploration of the Himalaya started only in the mid-1700's, when the British East India Company began extending its control over India and sending out expeditions to explore and map its frontiers. By the close of the century, a few of these expeditions had penetrated the Himalaya as far as Bhutan, Nepal, and Tibet. On the basis of their reports, the Surveyor General of Bengal, Captain James Rennell, was able to publish the first *Map of Hindoostan* in the 1780's.

The need for accurate knowledge of India's geography became more pressing in the years that followed, and soon a major project was underway. It was no less than the mapping of the entire sub-continent, including the 2,000-mile-long arc of mountains along India's northern frontier. This enormous undertaking was to occupy the men of the British Survey Corps for over a century. Moreover, it was to entail all the dangers and hardships of a lengthy military campaign, for the highlands of northern India were inhabited by warlike tribes who were willing to fight to the death to keep the white men out of their domains. The small parties of British soldiers

Captain James Rennell (1742-1830), the Surveyor General of Bengal. In 1783 he produced a notable *Map of Hindoostan*.

Below: a British army camp at Jytock Ridge in the 1840's. The military necessity for accurate maps led many survey officers to climb higher in the Himalaya as part of their job than mountaineers were then climbing in the Alps purely for the sport.

and surveyors who ventured into this uncharted enemy territory risked their lives on every foray. But the surveys were essential, and the work went on. By 1810, maps of the great valley of Nepal had been produced, the source of the Ganges accurately determined, and the first estimates of the most accessible Himalayan peaks made.

In 1823, the Indian Trigonometrical Survey, as the mapping of the sub-continent was called, gained a new surveyor general—Sir George Everest. He it was who first applied the "gridiron," or triangulation, system to large-scale map-making, and he who accurately established the India arc of the meridian (a line of known coordinates running from the southern tip of India to its northern frontier). Everest's innovations made it possible to calculate the relationship between any two geographical points in India. There was now a mathematical basis for determining the relative positions of the great Himalayan peaks, as well as their heights above sea level. To determine the height of an unknown peak, the surveyor traveled to an observation post whose height was known. From there he measured the peak's angle of elevation relative to a horizontal plane. From this he could determine the height of the peak above the observation post, and hence its height above sea level.

Above: Sir George Everest, for whom the highest mountain in the world was named. He was surveyor-general, and applied the triangulation system to the problem of large-scale mapping.

Using these highly scientific methods, the work of the Survey Corps proceeded rapidly, but it was still a dangerous undertaking. Sometimes it was even necessary for the surveyor to travel in disguise, as did the intrepid William Moorcroft, who made his first survey expedition in the garb of an Indian fakir or holy man.

Early in the 1800's, the frontiers of Nepal had been officially closed to foreigners, and until 1947 when this general policy of non-admittance was finally relaxed, Europeans were allowed inside the country only on rare occasions. During the 1800's, the other

Right: outsiders were not admitted in the Himalayan kingdoms. H. Y. Hearsey drew this sketch of himself and William Moorcroft disguised as Indian fakirs during their 1812 expedition to Tibet.

Below: a map taken from a report on the great Trigonometrical Survey shows the scale of the British undertaking. The Great Arc of the Meridian is the line of triangles running due north from the southern tip of India.

INDEX CHART
TO THE
GREAT TRIGONOMETRICAL SURVEY
OF
INDIA

Himalayan states, Tibet, Sikkim, and Bhutan, were only a little less reluctant than Nepal to permit foreigners within their borders. In the mid-1800's, as the British survey teams pushed ever deeper into the Himalaya, the distrust and defensiveness of India's northern neighbors increasingly hampered exploration. At last, finding that all Europeans were to be refused access to these northern regions, the British began training men from the hill tribes to pursue the work of the survey. These so-called "pundit-explorers" soon proved themselves not only hardy enough to withstand the rigors of high-altitude work, but also able to master, with remarkable rapidity, the intricacies of the refined measurement techniques then being used. One of the most famous of these pundits was a man called Nain Singh. On one occasion he made a 1,200 mile journey along the southern trade routes of Tibet to Lhasa and back, taking measurements and making notes all the way. The feat was all the more remarkable in that he had to keep these activities a complete secret from the Tibetan caravan merchants with whom he traveled.

It was another of these pundit-explorers who, in 1852, burst into the head office of the Indian Trigonometrical Survey and announced breathlessly that he had discovered the highest mountain in the world, a peak 29,002 feet high. The news was greeted with disbelief —could so high a mountain actually exist? But his calculations were found to be correct. And later, this mighty peak, number XV on the survey maps, was named Mount Everest, for the surveyor general who had done so much to make the mapping of the world's greatest mountains possible. To the Tibetan people, however, Everest is known as Chomolungma, "Goddess Mother of the Snows." The official height of Everest is set by the Indian government at 29,028 feet.

Below: the prime minister of Nepal, Jung Bahdour Koowar Ranajee. In spite of good personal relations between the British and the Nepalese, the borders of the kingdom remained closed to the British survey teams.

Nain Singh, one of the most famous of the hill tribe surveyors – the Pundits – penetrated deep into territory where Europeans were not admitted. As he traveled he took secret measurements.

As the systematic work of the Survey continued, countless surveyors and explorers, laden with heavy precision equipment, toiled up the peaks and passes of the Himalaya to take their measurements and make their reports. These hardy men had no intention of "mountaineering" in the sense in which that word was being used in the Alps, where the Golden Age of mountaineering was now underway. But while Swiss guides and English gentlemen were winning worldwide acclaim for their Alpine feats, Indian and Gurkha guides, officers, and soldiers of the Observers Corps of the British Army, and civilians employed by the Survey were frequently ascending peaks higher than anything in the "Playground of Europe" as part of their job.

For nearly a century, all the climbing done in the Himalaya had been strictly for scientific purposes—in addition to the surveyors, some few European naturalists and geologists had traveled to the Himalaya in the mid-1800's to carry out research. But the 1880's saw the arrival of a new breed of Himalayan climbers—men who saw in these towering ranges a field for adventure and conquest, rather than for research and discovery. The first European to climb in the Himalaya strictly for "sport and adventure," as he himself put it, was W. W. Graham who, in company with a Swiss guide named Joseph Imboden, traveled extensively in the mountains of Sikkim in 1883. Four years later, a young English lieutenant serving in India made a daring crossing of the perilous Mustagh Pass in the Karakoram range of northwest India. This adventurer, a man who never ceased to love the Himalaya, was Francis Younghusband. He later headed the committee that planned the first assaults on Everest.

The 1890's saw a rising tide in the number of specifically mountaineering expeditions to the Himalaya. In 1892, Martin Conway, already a veteran alpinist, led an expedition to the Karakoram range. In terms of sheer mountaineering, Conway's expedition succeeded in making only one major ascent, that of Pioneer Peak (22,600 feet). But in the course of his extensive exploration of the region, Conway made detailed maps of the Karakoram glaciers and kept careful records of the way in which high altitudes affected both human metabolic rates and the performance of delicate equipment. Both his maps and his notes on the effects of high altitudes were to prove invaluable to later expeditions.

One of the members of Conway's 1892 party was Charles Granville Bruce, a man who soon became one of the most famous and best loved figures in the whole history of Himalayan climbing. When he accompanied Conway to the Karakoram range he was a 26-year-old lieutenant in the British Army. He had already taken part in a number of survey and military expeditions in the Himalaya, and become a passionate addict of mountain climbing for its own sake. His every leave had been spent in the mountains, where he had come to know and love the hill peoples—the Gurkhas and Sherpas of the Kingdom of Nepal. As a result, his knowledge of Himalayan

Above: a drawing by a British survey officer, J. B. Bellasis, of himself conducting a survey from the camp.

Below: Martin Conway was one of the first "amateur" mountaineers in the Karakoram range. His maps and notes on the effects of the high altitude were to prove invaluable to later climbers.

conditions, terrain, languages, and peoples was greater than that of any other man of his time. "Charlie" Bruce was a huge and genial man, courageous and tremendously strong—Conway described him as the "goods-train" of the 1892 expedition. Tradition also has it that Bruce's preferred form of exercise when not mountaineering was running uphill before breakfast with a Gurkha guide under each arm! But that he was loved and revered by the Gurkhas is illustrated by the fact that even as late as the 1950's—years after his death—they were still relishing tales about "the great man Bruce" and his wonderful exploits.

Bruce was to have been part of the first attempt on a major Himalayan peak, Nanga Parbat (26,660 feet) in Kashmir in 1895, but was recalled to duty before the expedition could begin. The Nanga Parbat party was led by Albert F. Mummery, the famous pioneer of new routes and guideless climbing in the Alps. On the first attempt, Mummery and his party reached a height of 20,000 feet before being forced to retreat by the illness of one of the Gurkha guides. An indication of how little even an experienced Alpine climber understood the full realities of a Himalayan ascent is shown by the fact that Mummery believed that another night on the mountain would have been enough to get them up the remaining 6,000 feet. For the next try, the party agreed to separate and reconnoiter two different routes to the summit. Mummery and his two Gurkha guides were never seen again. Almost certainly they were swept away by an avalanche, an accident that may occur at any time in the high

Detail of map produced by Conway's 1892 expedition, this one showing the Baltoro Glacier. The painstaking accuracy of Conway's maps made them essential to later expeditions. This also maps Mount Godwin Austen, the Godwin Austen Glacier, and Mustagh Tower.

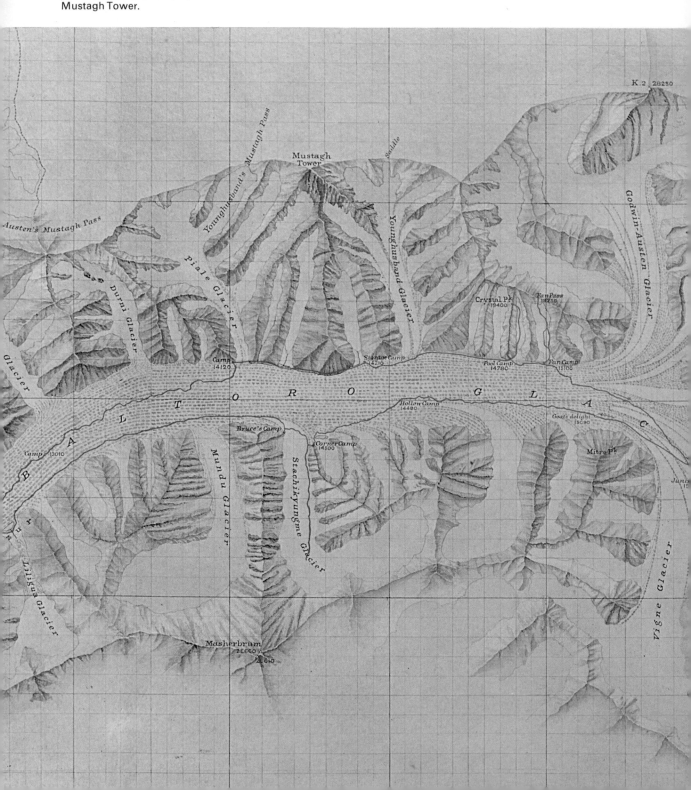

Right: members of the party which conquered Trisul in 1907. Second from the left is Dr. Tom Longstaff, who led the rapid ascent of this lofty peak, and Charles Granville Bruce (seated).

Himalaya. But just as certainly, Mummery had increased the likelihood of the disaster by applying Alpine tactics on the very much more hazardous surfaces of a Himalayan peak. There was still much to be learned about the true dimensions of the daunting Himalayan challenge.

Nevertheless, that great achievements were possible even in these early years of Himalayan mountaineering, was shown by Dr. Tom Longstaff's conquest of Trisul (23,360 feet) in northern India. Longstaff was as much a character in his own way as Charlie Bruce was in his. Small and wiry, with a beaked nose and a red moustache, he was an indefatigable mountaineer and, by the time he made his assault on Trisul, had already climbed in the Alps and the Caucasus and carried out extensive exploration in the mountains of Tibet and Nepal. His ascent of Trisul in 1907 was as much a feat of exploration as it was of mountaineering, for at that time there were no detailed maps of its surrounding glaciers. Luck was with him, however, for he hit on the very route that leads directly up the mountain's northeast face. But at 17,000 feet, Longstaff and his party began to suffer severely from the effects of high altitude. Soon they were gasping for breath and struggling against all the afflictions of mountain sickness—headache, nausea, weakness, and a frightening loss of willpower and concentration. Frozen and exhausted, they had just set up their camp when they were struck by the full force of a blinding blizzard. When at last it abated two days later, Longstaff, fearful of what a continued stay in the rarified atmosphere might do to himself and his men, decided to make a dash for the summit. In fact, his plan was to attempt the very thing on Trisul that Mummery had tried to do on Nanga Parbat—ascend 6,000 feet in one day! Amazingly, in spite of the intense cold, the whipping winds, and the difficulty of breathing, he and his two Swiss guides, Alexis and Henri Brocherel, succeeded in reaching the top after a climb of no more than 12 hours.

Theirs was a historic achievement, not only for the "rush" tactics employed on the final ascent, but for another reason as well. In the words of Kenneth Mason, author of the standard history of Himalayan exploration, and himself long attached to the Indian Survey, this was "the highest summit reached at that time, the height of which was actually known and about the ascent of which there was no doubt."

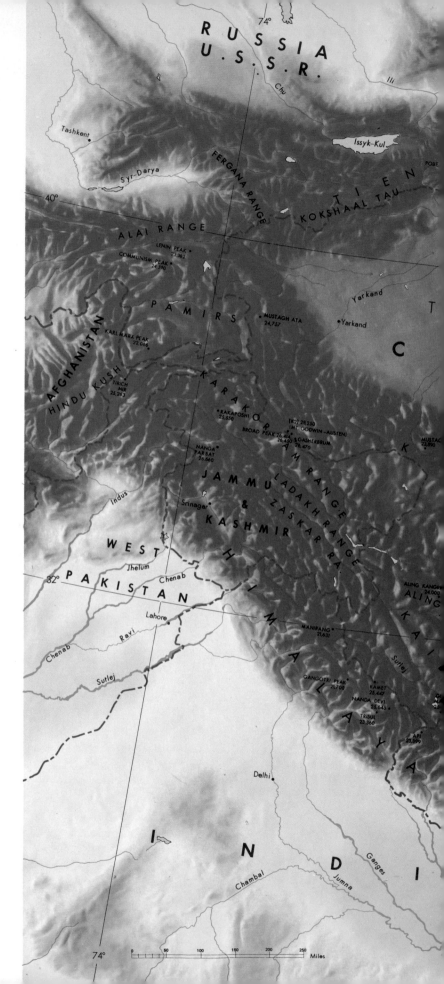

The Himalaya, the highest of the
world's mountain systems, in fact
consists of several parallel ranges.
They stretch in a 1500-mile curve
across southern Asia, from the
Pamirs in the west to the great bend
of the Brahmaputra River in the east.
Mount Everest, at 29,028 feet, the
highest mountain, is situated on the
frontier between Nepal and Tibet.

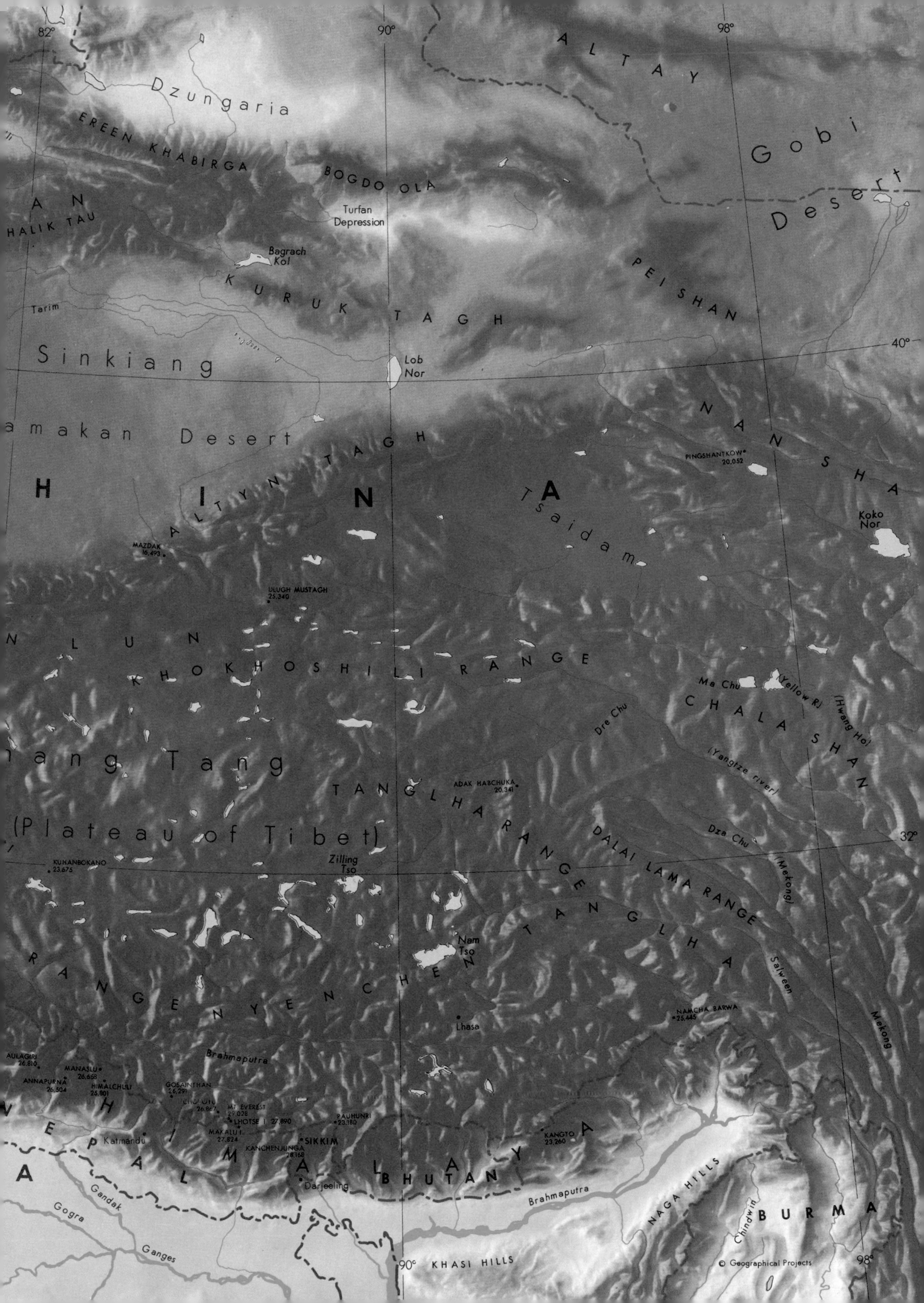

Dzungaria

ALTAY

G o b i

EREEN KHABIRGA

BOGDO OLA

PEI SHAN

Desert

AN

HALIK TAU

Turfan
Depression

Bagrach
Kol

KURUK TAGH

40°

Tarim

Lob
Nor

Sinkiang

NANSHA

N A N S H A

PINGSHANTKOW•
20,052

amakan Desert

ALTYN TAGH

N

A

Tsaidam

Koko
Nor

H

MAZDAK
16,493 •

ULUGH MUSTAGH
25,340

N L U N

KHOKHOSHILI RANGE

Ma Chu

(Yellow R)

CHALA SHAN

Dre Chu

(Hwang Ho)

ang Tang

(Yangtze river)

TANGLHA RANGE

ADAK HABCHUKA
20,341 •

Dza Chu

DALAI LAMA RANGE

(Mekong)

32°

(Plateau of Tibet)

KUHANBOKANO
• 23,675

Zilling
Tso

TANGLHA

RANGE

Nam
Tso

NAMCHA BARWA
• 25,445

Salween

N Y E N C H E N

•Lhasa

Mekong

AULAGRI
26,810

Brahmaputra

MANASLU•
26,658

ANNAPURNA
26,504

HIMALCHULI
25,801

GOSAINTHAN
26,291

P

CHO YU 10
26,867•

MT. EVEREST
29,028

PAUHUNRI
23,180

KANGTO
23,260

A

Katmandu

MAKALU•
27,824

LHOTSE I 27,890

H I M A L A Y A

SIKKIM

E

Darjeeling

KANCHENJUNGA
28,168

BHUTAN

NAGA HILLS

Chindwin

BURMA

A

Gogra

Gandak

Brahmaputra

Ganges

90°

KHASI HILLS

98°

© Geographical Projects

Left: Mrs. Fanny Bullock Workman at the door of her tent in a camp in the Karakoram range. With her husband, Dr. William Hunter Workman, she climbed extensively in the Himalaya at the turn of the century. Unfortunately, many of their records have since been found to be inaccurate.

The Duke of the Abruzzi (1873-1933), of the Royal House of Savoy. An enthusiastic mountaineer, he led a large expedition to conquer the mighty Mount Godwin Austen. The expedition was unsuccessful, but reached a height of some 24,000 feet.

These carefully chosen words show the problems not so much of climbing in the Himalaya, but of verifying the claims, sometimes made in good faith, of those who had done so. Perhaps no claims were more difficult to verify than those made by an American husband and wife team who climbed extensively in the Himalaya at the turn of the century. Dr. William Hunter Workman and his wife, Fanny Bullock Workman, made their first expedition to the Karakoram range in 1899. Both on this, and on subsequent expeditions, they were accompanied by competent guides, and succeeded in scaling a number of peaks. But just which peaks, and how high they were, was open to debate, for the Workmans did not consider it necessary to consult the Indian Survey before making their claims. They were prone to be inaccurate in their noting of the exact height and locations of the mountains they explored, and frequently claimed to have made the first ascents of peaks that had been climbed before. To their credit, however, it must be said that on their last expedition to the Karakoram range in 1912, they did take with them an expert cartographer, and with his help produced several useful maps of the region's glaciers.

Another notable contribution to Himalayan exploration was made in 1909, by an expedition led by the famous Italian mountaineer, the Duke of the Abruzzi. Behind him he already had two remarkable expeditions: the ascent of Alaska's Mount Saint Elias in 1897, and the exploration of Uganda's Ruwenzori range in 1906. In the year 1909, he assembled another large and highly professional group of scientists and mountaineers, and set off for the Karakoram range. His objective was Mount Godwin Austen (28,250 feet) on the China-Kashmir border. This mountain, second only to Everest in height, was named for the surveyor Henry Godwin Austen. It is also known as Dapsang (its local name) and K2, the number given it during the survey. Filippo de Filippi, the naturalist on the Duke's expedition,

has described it as a "quadrangular pyramid," made up of four
immense ridges which soar upward from the southwest, the
northwest, the southeast, and the northeast. The Duke's party
reconnoitered all four approaches. In addition, they thoroughly
mapped the region surrounding the massive Godwin Austen glacier
that sweeps down the mountain's south face. The party made a
heroic attempt to reach the summit via a narrow ridge on the south
face, but were forced to retreat because they could find no place on
the knife-edge of the ridge to establish a camp. Before turning back,
however, they did reach a height of some 24,600 feet on the ridge.
In their honor, the approach was thereafter known as the Abruzzi
Ridge.

One of the members of the Duke's party was the famed mountaineer-photographer Vittorio Sella. In the course of the expedition
he took some of the most valuable, and certainly the most beautiful
photographs of his career. His numerous pictures of every side of
the world's second highest mountain were used in planning every
later expedition to the peak.

By the close of the first decade of the 1900's, a score of daring
attempts had been made on giants of the Himalaya. As yet, only
two peaks over 23,000 feet had been climbed: Trisul (23,360 feet)
by Tom Longstaff, in 1907, and Pauhunri (23,180 feet) by Dr. A. M.
Kellas, in 1910. But many of the mountaineers who had pitted themselves against the monarchs of the Himalaya had reached heights of
20,000 and more, and all of them had done so armed only with the
traditional equipment of the alpinist: crampons, ice-ax, rope, and
woolen clothing. Encouraged by the success of these pioneers, men
began to dream of conquering Everest itself. The dream was kept
alive throughout the grim years of World War I, and, in 1921, the
first Everest expedition set off to reconnoiter this, the mightiest of
all the world's mountains.

Confronting the Himalayan Giants

9

Before the British expedition to Everest in 1921, no European had ever even reached the base of the mountain, let alone explored its heights. Situated on the frontier between Nepal and Tibet, Everest had long been inaccessible to Westerners because both Nepal and Tibet strictly forbade foreigners within their borders. The only European who had ever succeeded in getting anywhere near the mountain was a young British officer named John Noel. Noel had done some Alpine climbing as a boy. When he was stationed in India in 1913, he spent his first leaves exploring the foothills of the Himalaya. The mystery of the forbidden lands beyond the mountains intrigued him, and he was soon engaged in trying to find a way through to Tibet. Time after time he was turned back by Tibetan soldiers, but at last he located an unguarded pass 20,000 feet high, and managed to penetrate deep into the kingdom of Tibet before being found out and forced to make his way back. It was only after returning to India that he learned that he had come within 40 miles of Everest—closer than any European had ever been before.

After the war, Captain Noel was one of the men chosen to take part in the first expedition to Everest. An Everest Committee had been formed, and the Dalai Lama of Tibet was at last persuaded to permit the expedition to enter his country. The ruler of Nepal, however, would not relent, even for so momentous a project as the first exploration of Everest. As a result, when the expedition at last set out in 1921, it was forced to make a long detour around Nepal before it could arrive at its destination, the valleys at the foot of Everest's glaciers.

Structurally, Everest is an immense pyramid, having three massive faces and three major ridges which soar up to the summit from the north, south, and west. The longest of these huge buttresses is the north ridge. After a thorough reconnaissance, the members of the 1921 expedition concluded that the only feasible route to the summit was by way of this ridge. The ascent plan they suggested was to climb the mighty East Rongbuk Glacier to a pass on the north ridge called the North Col, and from there to proceed along the

The main base camp of the 1922 Everest expedition, on the northern approach to the mountain. The photograph was taken and colored by Captain John Noel, photographer on the 1922 and 1924 expeditions.

N. E. Should
1st Rece

Camp

main body of the ridge to the summit. As far as they could determine, the chief problem was to reach the North Col itself, which lies at the top of a sheer ice-wall nearly 1,800 feet high.

But whatever purely structural problems the ascent of Everest might entail, one thing was certain: its climbers would have to endure high-altitude conditions more extreme than any mountaineer had ever faced before. Only a comparatively few men had as yet climbed above 20,000 feet, and no one knew what the effects of prolonged work above 25,000 feet might be. Everest was over 29,000 feet, and many people seriously doubted whether the human body could withstand the effects of severe oxygen deprivation at such heights. A kind of oxygen apparatus for use at high altitudes had already made its appearance, but it was still very primitive—heavy, ungainly, and frequently unreliable. Few mountaineers trusted it enough to burden themselves with it on long climbs. Moreover, many mountaineers of this time regarded the use of so artificial a climbing aid with disapproval. Nonetheless, oxygen equipment was taken on the second Everest expedition in 1922.

The 1922 expedition was led by Charles Bruce (at that time a brigadier general in the British Army) and included a number of such highly experienced climbers as John Noel, Tom Longstaff, and Dr. T. H. Somervell. This was to be no mere reconnaissance mission, but rather an all-out assault on the mountain. Accordingly, Bruce moved the team up in easy stages, a strategy which he hoped would conserve the men's energies and give them sufficient time to acclimatize before the final assault. But despite these precautions, the 1922 expedition failed to gain its objective. The first assault team, having reached a height of 26,700 feet, was forced down by the painful difficulty of breathing in the rarified air. The second, equipped with the cumbersome oxygen apparatus, managed to reach a height of 27,230 feet before being defeated by winds so fierce that the climbers could hardly stand upright. The third and final assault party had barely reached the Col when it was struck by an avalanche. Seven Sherpa porters lost their lives in this tragic accident, and the expedition was brought to a halt.

Despite disaster and defeat, the 1922 expedition produced two

Noel's map of Everest's north face. Until Nepal opened her borders in 1947, this was the only possible way to the summit. The base camp, at the bottom right, was at 16,000 feet. The route up lay along the East Rongbuk Glacier, with a chain of depot camps established at 6-mile intervals. At the head of the glacier, at 21,000 feet, was the advance base camp on a snow field beneath a sheer ice-wall.

positive results. First, the use of oxygen was now seen to be an absolute necessity at heights over 26,000 feet. Using it, men had been able to climb higher—and camp higher—than ever before. Second, the true value of the Sherpa porters was now fully recognized. Tough and energetic, they had proved themselves capable of carrying heavy packs to heights of over 25,000 feet. Moreover, they had shown themselves to be natural mountaineers in the truest sense of the word.

The Sherpas belong to a small group of people who inhabit the mountain frontier between Nepal and Tibet. Small, but exceptionally hardy, most are farmers, but some are mountain tradesmen, accustomed from early youth to carrying heavy goods over the high passes of the Himalaya. For this reason they make superb expedition porters. But perhaps even more important than their strength and endurance on a Himalayan expedition is their remarkable temperament. They are a courageous and optimistic people, capable of great feats of heroism, and have a fine sense of humor and a genial tolerance for the ways of foreigners. From the outset, the Sherpas understood the seeming madness of risking life and limb to reach the summit of a mountain. Many of the Sherpas soon became competent mountaineers in their own right, and proved themselves climbing companions as skilled as any of the Swiss guides of the Golden Age. In the history of Himalayan mountaineering, the courage, devotion, and loyalty of the Sherpas have become legendary. On many expeditions, Sherpas have risked their own lives to save those of their employers. And on more than one tragic occasion, they have sacrificed their lives rather than abandon a "sahib" in trouble.

Sherpas made up the majority of the porters on the Everest expedition of 1924. Led by Colonel E. F. Norton, the expedition included some of the finest climbers of the day. Chief among them was a young man named George Leigh Mallory, who had taken part in both the 1921 and the 1922 expeditions. Mallory was a schoolteacher by profession, but had long been an ardent climber, and was well-known in mountaineering circles. All who knew him spoke of his overriding obsession with Everest. From the moment he first saw it, Everest became "his" mountain. Ultimately, the names of Mallory and Mount Everest were destined to become as closely linked in mountaineering legend as those of Edward Whymper and the Matterhorn.

Colonel Norton had worked out a careful plan for the 1924 attack on Everest. After several weeks of staged acclimatization, the party was to work in teams of two, the fittest men working without oxygen, the others with it. The assault was to be made, as before, via the North Col. The party established its base camp on the East Rongbuk Glacier on April 29, and began to prepare for the assault.

The first two attempts were defeated by savage blizzards. Each took weeks of grueling effort, and the men's energies were sorely depleted. But the monsoons were due to begin soon, and when they

Above: Charles Granville Bruce, leader of the 1922 Everest expedition. Bruce had been greatly loved by the Gurkhas whom he had commanded, and the stories of his strength and courage became folk tales of the mountain people. Thirty years later W. H. Murray was being asked how he was. Murray reported that he hadn't the heart to tell the people that Bruce, in fact, was dead.

The Sherpas, who live in the frontier region between Nepal and Tibet, are accustomed to carrying heavy loads at high altitudes—experience which prepared them well for the part they increasingly played in expeditions, first as skilled porters and then as fellow climbers with the foreigners.

Above: some of the members of the 1924 Everest expedition at the base camp. Standing, left to right, are Irvine, Mallory, Norton (leader), Odell, and MacDonald. Seated, left to right, Shebbeare, Bruce, Somervell, and Beetham.

Left: George Leigh Mallory, the most famous mountaineer of his day. His reason for climbing Everest—"because it is there"—whether he meant it as a serious remark or not, has become the classic rationale for mountaineering.

did, all hope of continuing would have to be abandoned. With time running out, there was nothing to do but strike again at once.

Mallory and Charles Bruce's son, Geoffrey Bruce, went up first and established a camp above the North Col at 25,000 feet. The next team, Norton and Somervell, took over from there. After establishing Camp VI, at 26,800 feet, they made a heroic effort to reach the summit without oxygen. At 28,000 feet, however, breathing became almost unbearably painful, and they were forced to turn back. It was clear that oxygen would have to be used in the ascent of the final 1,000 feet. The third and last assault team was to be Noel Odell and 22-year-old Andrew Irvine. Odell, however, had taken longer to acclimatize than the others, and was not fit enough to undertake the climb. Mallory, still very strong and more than ever determined to conquer "his" mountain, was chosen to take Odell's place.

Early on June 6, Mallory and Irvine, with 30-pound oxygen packs

Mallory, Irvine, and three Sherpas
setting off on one of the stages of their
assault on Everest. Mallory and Irvine
disappeared on the last stage and their
bodies were never found.

strapped to their backs, left their companions at Camp IV, a little
below the North Col, and set off for the summit. Odell stationed
himself at Camp VI, about 3,000 feet below the summit, to watch
for them. Mist obscured the upper reaches of the peak for most of
the morning, but at 12:50 P.M., the swirling clouds parted, and he
caught a glimpse of the two tiny figures. They were only 800 feet
from the top and still edging their way forward along the ridge. It
could not be long now, he thought, before they reached the summit.

Odell returned to Camp IV where, throughout the long moonlit
night, he watched in vain for some sign of Mallory and Irvine. The
next day he climbed alone to Camp V, spent the night there, and set
off at dawn to search for them. Camp VI was just as he had seen it
two days before—empty. He continued upward until he could go no
farther, and at last, all hope gone, he returned to Camp VI, where
he laid out the two climbers' abandoned blankets in the shape of a T.

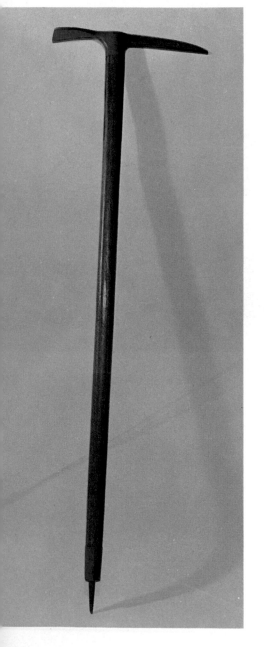

The ice-ax, which must have belonged to either Mallory or Irvine, which Wyn Harris found lying at 27,600 feet.

Far below, his teammates saw the signal through their telescopes and read its tragic message: "no trace." Ninety years later, an ice-ax was found 60 feet below the final crest at a height of about 27,600 feet. Whether it was Mallory's or Irvine's is not certain. All that is known is that somewhere, within yards of their cherished goal, the two men lost their footing and plummeted to their deaths.

There were to be no less than four more British attempts on Everest before World War II: in 1933, 1935, 1936, and 1938. All four were made from the North Col on the Tibetan side of the mountain. All failed, and all confirmed the crucial part played by the severe weather conditions on Everest's heights—above all, the howling winds that seemed bent either on tearing the climber from the side of the mountain or driving him back with sprays of blinding snow.

While the decade of the 1930's did not witness a successful assault on Everest, it did see heroic achievements elsewhere in the Himalaya. In 1931, a British expedition led by Frank Smythe conquered Kamet (25,447 feet), in northern India. And, in the next eight years, no less than nine peaks of over 22,000 feet were climbed by teams from Britain, Switzerland, Germany, Japan, and the United States.

American mountaineering in the Himalaya began with a daring expedition to a lofty Chinese mountain, Minya Konka. Situated near Tibet, in the Chinese province of Szechwan, the mountain is part of an outlying spur of the Himalayan system. In 1932, when the American expedition set out to explore it, little was known about Minya Konka. Some believed that it might even be higher than Everest itself. In fact, at 24,900 feet, Minya Konka proved to be about four-fifths of a mile lower than Everest. Nevertheless, this first ascent of the peak was an extremely arduous undertaking. Led by Richard Burdsall, the climb was made during late October in the very teeth of a savage storm. For this reason alone, the climb was a remarkable feat. More important still, it aroused American interest in Himalayan climbing.

The highest mountain scaled during the 1930's was northern India's Nanda Devi (25,645 feet), perhaps the most romantic of all Himalayan peaks. According to legend, it is the sanctuary of the goddess Nanda, who fled to its icy turrets to escape the machinations of an evil prince. Certainly the mountain strikingly resembles a fortress, for it is surrounded on all sides by a towering wall of peaks

Right: the letter Mallory sent down to Noel from the bivouac at 27,000 feet, making arrangements for Noel to film their progress across the skyline. The time should have read "8 A.M."

Dear Noel
We'll probably start early to-morrow (8th) in order to have clear weather. It won't be too early to start looking out for us either crossing the rockband under the pyramid or going up skyline at 8.0 p.m.

Yrs ever
G. Mallory

During the 1930's many expeditions were mounted to other parts of the Himalaya. These climbers are members of the 1936 expedition led by Paul Bauer to Mount Siniolchu, called the most beautiful mountain in the world.

Left: a drawing made in 1851 by Henry Ambrose Oldfield of Nanda Devi, the sacred mountain. In legend it is the sanctuary of the Indian goddess Nanda.

Below: one of the mixed blessings of Himalayan climbing is the necessity for long approach marches to get to the mountains—but sometimes the march is through beautiful forests.

and ridges. Within the outer wall there is a second ring of mountains known as the Inner Sanctuary. This second ring was first seen in 1905 by Tom Longstaff who, in the course of exploring the region, climbed to the rim of the outer wall. Longstaff tried, and failed, to gain the Inner Sanctuary, but he did locate the only possible way in: the gorge of the Rishi Ganga River. Perilously steep, the crumbling rock walls of the gorge plunge thousands of feet down to the torrential waters below. The gorge itself is difficult enough to challenge the skills of the most expert mountaineer.

In 1934, a small party consisting of Eric Shipton, H. W. Tilman, and three Sherpas made their way through the magically beautiful forest region of the lower Himalayan valleys, and began a full-scale exploration of the Nanda Devi Ring. After five months of careful reconnoitering and hazardous climbing, they succeeded in forcing a passage through the Rishi Gorge and reached the Inner Sanctuary. Here they surveyed Nanda Devi's slopes from the secluded valleys at its base, and worked out possible routes to its summit. The party was too small to attempt an ascent of the mountain itself, but the groundwork was laid for a later expedition.

Two years later, an Anglo-American team, led jointly by a Welshman, T. Graham Brown, and an American, Dr. Charles Houston, set off to make the first ascent of Nanda Devi. Among the four Americans in the party was Arthur Emmons, who had taken part in the ascent of Minya Konka in 1932. Among the four Englishmen were Noel Odell, who had been on the tragic 1924 Everest expedition, and H. W. Tilman, who, with Shipton, had reconnoitered Nanda Devi in 1934. Ironically, Shipton himself was unable to join the expedition, because he was engaged in the 1936 attempt on Everest.

The climb was an exceptionally difficult one in many respects. Apart from the seasoned climber Pasang Kikuli, the Sherpas of the party were inexperienced. And when they were confronted by a difficult crossing of the Rishi Ganga, the majority of them flatly refused to go any farther. This left the party with a mere handful of porters to carry all the food and equipment necessary for the long siege on the mountain. The only solution was for each of the American and British members of the team to assume the role of carrier as well as climber. Even so, it took countless trips by both "sahibs" and Sherpas to bring everything through the gorge and up to the base camp at 15,000 feet.

By the time they had reached 21,000 feet, the party had suffered further setbacks. Frostbite, snow-blindness, and mountain sickness had forced two of the Americans and the two remaining Sherpas to drop out, and blizzards had halted the progress of the others time after time. But although there were now only six men left to make the final assault, and although the energies of these six were daily being drained by the work of ferrying up their supplies, the four Britons and two Americans were more determined than ever to succeed.

At last they reached 23,000 feet, and Odell and Houston were chosen to make the final assault. But the night before they were to set off, Houston was taken severely ill with food-poisoning. Tilman was chosen to take his place. He and Odell started for the summit at dawn the next day. The expedition carried no oxygen equipment, so the two men had to rely on their reserves of strength and on their determination to keep them going through the increasingly rarified air. Each step forward had to be followed by five or six deep breaths, and their progress was extremely slow. They ploughed through knee-deep powdery snow, ascended a steep ice-wall, and narrowly avoided being swept away by an avalanche. And then, at long last, they reached the final crest of the ridge and strode forward to the mountain's highest point. It was a moment of great triumph but, as Tilman wrote later, "After the first joy in victory came a feeling of sadness that the mountain had succumbed, that the proud head of the goddess was bowed."

But if Nanda Devi could be humbled, it seemed that another great Himalayan peak, Nanga Parbat, could not. In fact this 26,660-foot peak became notorious during the 1930's for the series of disasters which prevented party after party from reaching its summit.

Nanga Parbat is situated in northwest Kashmir, a few miles from the Indus River. Structurally, the mountain resembles Everest—one long major ascending ridge, with a minor peak halfway along. By far the most accessible approach to the summit is via the north face. But, because the ice and snow on the north face is liable to avalanche at frequent intervals, the route to the first snow ridge must be circuitous. This route has been described as "twice as high as the North Col [on Everest] climb, three times as dangerous, and four times as long in point of time." It was on Nanga Parbat that Albert F. Mummery, ignorant of the real problem of Himalayan climbing, lost his life in 1895.

In 1934, a large and highly professional German expedition, led by Willy Merkl, set off to master Nanga Parbat. Merkl had led

another expedition to the mountain two years before, and was well acquainted with the immense difficulties of both the route and the weather conditions on the mountain. The 1934 expedition was rather badly organized, but under his vigorous leadership, it went very well in its early stages. After several weeks of steady climbing and camp-making, 5 Germans and 11 Sherpas reached the "Silver Saddle," a deep depression in the final ridge some 2,000 feet from the summit. Success seemed near at hand. Then, suddenly, the mountain seemed to lash out at the men with diabolical ferocity. A

Above: Willy Merkl, second from the right, leaving Munich in 1934 at the start of the journey to Nanga Parbat, the mountain he hoped to conquer, and on the slopes of which he perished.

Right: camp being set up by the 1937 Nanga Parbat expedition, with the tents sunk partially in the snow for extra protection. The camp was later completely obliterated by an avalanche that struck in the night, killing all 16 climbers who were sleeping there. The negative of this photograph was found when the camp was dug out by would-be rescuers.

raging storm swept down on them and imprisoned all 16 of the advance party in their tents. On the second day, although the blizzard had not let up, Merkl was forced to order a retreat. They were 4,000 feet above the next supply camp and their food was fast running out.

In the terrible few days that followed, all but 7 of the 16 members of the advance party perished in the attempt to reach the safety of the lower camp. Those who survived staggered into the camp one by one, hollow-eyed, frostbitten, and almost dead from exhaustion.

The plains of Katmandu, dominated by the Annapurna range of mountains. It was Annapurna itself which the 1950 French expedition resolved to conquer.

The support party from the lower camp made repeated, frantic efforts to locate those still on the mountain, but were beaten back each time by the storm. On one occasion they made out three tiny figures on the ridge high above them, and even thought they heard a far-off cry for help. Then the blizzard closed in once more and, weeping, they were forced to retreat. The last man to come down from the ridge alive was the Sherpa Ang Tsering. He had been with Merkl and another Sherpa, Gay-Lay, when Merkl collapsed. Gay-Lay had sent Ang Tsering ahead to try and reach the camp. He himself, he said, would remain with the fallen leader. And indeed he did remain, and perished with Merkl in the storm.

German mountaineers were determined to avenge the tragic deaths of their compatriots by conquering this deadly mountain. But in 1937, when the next German expedition made an assault on the mountain, another awesome disaster occurred. In the middle of the night of June 14, a sudden and tremendous avalanche shook the mountain and thundered down on the 7 Germans and 9 Sherpas asleep in their tents. All 16 perished.

Two more German expeditions (one of them led by the great climber Paul Bauer) tried and failed, to reach Nanga Parbat's summit in the late 1930's. But these repeated assaults on the peak had made Nanga Parbat as much "Germany's mountain" as Everest, after many English expeditions, had become "Britain's mountain." And, ultimately, in the great period of Himalayan mountaineering that began after World War II, it was to be a Briton who conquered Everest, and a German who conquered Nanga Parbat. But even before these two great peaks were mastered, another Himalayan monarch—the great Annapurna—was to be the site of a thrilling and historic conquest.

There are only 14 mountains in the world over 26,000 feet high, and Annapurna, in north-central Nepal, is eleventh on this list of giants. In 1950, a French expedition, led by Maurice Herzog, traveled to the Himalaya with the intention of climbing either Annapurna or Dhaulagiri (which at 26,810 feet, is the seventh highest of the mighty 14). After lengthy reconnaissance, they chose to make their assault on Annapurna (26,504 feet).

Louis Lachenal, suffering badly from oxygen starvation and frostbite, is helped down the slopes of Annapurna, exhausted but victorious. Although the descent was harrowing, Lachenal has since said that he did not regret it.

The early stages of the climb went well, and, on June 3, 1950, Herzog set off with Louis Lachenal for the top. They had no oxygen equipment and, as they climbed steadily higher, they had to fight off wave after wave of giddiness and loss of concentration. But they kept struggling forward, and at last, gasping and exhausted, they gained the topmost point. Here they planted the French flag and took pictures of each other. Then they started back down. As they did so, Herzog, his senses numbed by severe oxygen deprivation, somehow managed to lose his gloves.

The loss of Herzog's gloves proved to be only the first of a series of castastrophes that nearly turned triumph into tragedy. Herzog and Lachenal, together with Lionel Terray and Gaston Rébuffat (who had waited for them at the highest camp), were caught in a howling blizzard as they started down together. They were unable to find the next camp, and had to spend the night in a shallow crevasse. Desperately tired but fearful of freezing to death in their sleep, the four huddled together and tried to warm their feet by putting them in their rucksacks. In the morning, the boots they had taken off were buried in the snow. They searched frantically for them, clawing through the snow on their hands and knees, but it took an hour to locate all four pairs—an hour that sealed the fate of the summit team's already badly frostbitten feet.

Miraculously, the four men, by now snowblind as well as frostbitten and pitifully weak, were found later in the day by a rescue party from below. With their teammates' help, they somehow managed to stagger down to the safety of the next camp. There, the expedition doctor gave Herzog and Lachenal massive injections of novaine acetychlorodine to stimulate the flow of blood in their frostbitten limbs. Both men were carried on the backs of the party's devoted Sherpas all the way back to India. There, after a series of operations—in which all of Herzog's fingers and some of both his and Lachenal's toes had to be amputated—the two fearless conquerors of Annapurna slowly recovered their health.

It was a terrible price to pay for victory, but neither Herzog nor Lachenal regretted it. They had become the first men to master a peak over 26,000 feet high, and it was a triumph of historic proportions. It was their climb that launched a whole new era in the history of Himalayan mountaineering, an era which has come to be called "The New Golden Age."

The first of the giants conquered. Maurice Herzog, leader of the 1950 expedition that climbed Annapurna, stands at the summit at the moment of victory, photographed by his companion, Louis Lachenal. They were the first to master a peak over 26,000 feet high, and their achievement began the New Golden Age of climbing.

The New Golden Age

10

Left: the immensity of the Himalayan challenge is dramatically demonstrated by this picture of climbers moving determinedly past an enormous chasm in the Western Cwm, the long, narrow ice valley which proved to offer the best route to the summit of Everest.

Below: the British climber Eric Shipton suggested that the best route up Everest was through the Khumbu Glacier, up the Icefall, and across the crevasse to the Western Cwm. These porters were an essential part of the 1953 expedition, which followed that exact route.

That the 1950 ascent of Annapurna had indeed been the herald of great things to come was emphatically confirmed on a warm spring day three years later. On that day, May 29, 1953, the world reverberated with the breathtaking news that Mount Everest had been conquered.

The story of the conquest of Everest, perhaps the most historic event in mountaineering history, goes back to the years immediately following World War II, after Nepal agreed in 1947 to open its frontiers to foreign expeditions. This change in Nepal's policy made it possible for mountaineers to begin exploration of the southern approach to the mountain. In 1951, a British expedition led by Eric Shipton made a thorough reconnaissance of this approach, and located what was to prove the most practical route to the summit. This is the opening, in the *western* ridge of the mountain, through which the vast Khumbu Glacier descends. Farther up, the glacier becomes a steep wall of ice. And at the top of this icefall is a deep crevasse, which separates it from a long, narrow, ice-filled valley called the Western Cwm. At the head of this valley is another ridge, with the summit of Everest at one end, and the summits of its sister peaks, Lhotse I and II, at the other. In between, where the ridge sinks down, is the South Col. The plan of attack suggested by Shipton's party was to climb the Khumbu Icefall and cross the

Above: Raymond Lambert with Tenzing Norgay. They climbed to 750 feet below the summit before being forced back on the 1952 Swiss attempt. Below: John Hunt, the brilliant leader and organizer who led the successful British assault on Everest. His fine leadership helped produce the victory.

crevasse to the Western Cwm; to continue up the Cwm to Everest's southeast ridge; to attain the South Col from that ridge; and, from the South Col, to stage a final assault directly up to Everest's summit.

In 1952, two successive Swiss expeditions attempted to reach the summit by way of this southern route. On the first attempt, two of the party, Raymond Lambert and the skilled Sherpa climber Tenzing Norgay, came within 750 feet of the summit before being forced to retreat by the paralyzing effects of high altitude. They were equipped with oxygen cylinders, but the effort required to manipulate the flow of air was almost as energy-consuming as climbing without the aid of oxygen. Nonetheless, they had succeeded in establishing a new height record—and this, after spending a sleepless night at 27,500 feet, without sleeping-bags or a stove to ward off the sub-zero cold.

Tenzing and Lambert attempted the final assault again on the second Swiss expedition later that year. Once more, they were defeated by the wind, the cold, and the rarified atmosphere of the heights. But despite their defeat, the Swiss expedition had achieved two important things. First, it had carried out the heroic chore of forging the route. Second, it had demonstrated that even heavily laden porters could make the ascent by this route as far as the slopes directly below the South Col.

In 1953, a British expedition set off to tackle the great peak. In a sense it was a do-or-die mission, for strong Swiss and French teams were already being assembled for Everest assaults in 1954 and 1955. If the British were ever to master "their" mountain, it must be now. Heading the 1953 team was Colonel John Hunt, a man already widely known for his exceptional powers of leadership and organization. Among the 13 other members of the party were three scientists, Tom Bourdillon, Michael Westmacott, and George Band; three doctors, Charles Evans, Michael Ward, and Griffith Pugh; two teachers, Wilfrid Noyce and the New Zealander George Lowe; a professional beekeeper, Edmund Hillary (also from New Zealand); an army officer Charles Wylie; a travel agent, Alfred Gregory; a photographer, Tom Stobart; and the Sherpa *sirdar* or headman, Tenzing Norgay, now a full-fledged expedition member.

As on all major climbs, the ascent party was supported by an army of porters, and the assault had to be methodically prepared for by the establishment of supply depots from the Base Camp, at 18,000 feet, to Camp VIII, on the South Col at 26,000 feet. Hunt brought the expedition up in easy stages, giving both climbers and porters ample time to acclimatize as they progressed from camp to camp. The route up the Khumbu Icefall proved particularly arduous, a veritable obstacle course of chasms and *séracs* (ice-pillars), which soon acquired such nicknames as Hellfire Alley and the Atom Bomb area. As far as the head of the Western Cwm, Hunt followed the route pioneered by the Swiss. But from there, he forged a different route, via the Lhotse Glacier, to the South Col. It was a more indirect approach, but far safer. When Camp VIII had been set up on the Col, two final assault parties were chosen; the first to be Bourdillon and Evans, the second, Hillary and Tenzing.

On May 26, the first pair set off early, and by early afternoon were in sight of the final crest. But here, close as they were to success, the two were forced to turn back by insufficient reserves of oxygen. They were using a new type of oxygen apparatus designed specifically for the expedition. But although it was vastly superior to anything used before, it was still prone to develop defects.

On May 27, a high wind sprang up and storm clouds scudded across the sky. Hillary and Tenzing, poised for their attack on the summit, feared that the weather might close in and put an end to their hopes. But on May 28, the weather suddenly cleared, and they started off. Previously, bivouac equipment had been taken up to a height of 27,900 feet, and it was here that Tenzing and Hillary spent the night. Their tent was pitched on a narrow ledge hacked in the steep slope of the ice-covered ridge. They slept only fitfully, for at that height sleep was only possible with the use of oxygen, and their precious supply had to be conserved for the next day's effort.

The morning dawned bright and clear, and they set off at 6:30 A.M. The surface of the snow on the ridge before them was treacherous, and they were frequently forced off the crest itself by massive cornices of snow. When this happened, they had to inch their way along the sheer ice-wall of the ridge until they had

Part of the plan for the conquest of Everest included a higher base camp than ever before, but this meant long grueling climbs for men burdened with supplies, bringing them up through the hazards of the Icefall.

Hillary checks over Tenzing's oxygen equipment as they set out on the last leg of the climb to be first men to stand at the top of the world. Hillary later said he spent much of the climb calculating and recalculating what their oxygen needs would be.

passed the difficult point on the crest. At one point, the oxygen in their cylinders froze up, but they succeeded in getting it started again. As Hillary wrote later, his thoughts were preoccupied with their ever-dwindling supply of oxygen during the whole of the climb: would they have enough, he wondered with increasing anxiety, to get them there *and* back?

On and on they struggled, gaining only one foot per minute. Suddenly there loomed before them a 40-foot pinnacle of rock. One of its sides was a continuation of the sheer wall of the ridge, and from the other there swept outward a huge wing of snow. For a moment, it seemed that this staring face of rock was going to prove one obstacle too many. But perhaps there *was* a way past it. Hillary stepped forward and wedged himself into the narrow gap between the rock and the treacherous white cornice. Slowly, he began hauling himself up. It was like climbing a chimney, one side of which was liable to fall away at any moment. Fortunately, it held until he could force his way to the top and throw down a rope for Tenzing.

It was not long after overcoming this obstacle that the two found themselves taking their final steps to the summit. There, at the top

of the world, they heartily congratulated each other. After resting briefly, they took photographs, and dug a small hole in the snow in which they placed two objects: a little crucifix given by Hunt to Hillary to leave at the summit, and a packet of chocolate brought by Tenzing as a gift to the Buddhist gods.

Their stay at the top of Everest lasted only 15 minutes. It was essential to return before their oxygen ran out. By 2 P.M. they were back at their final bivouac. And late that afternoon they reached the lower camp, where they were met by the support party.

When Hunt, at a still-lower camp, first saw the party of descending climbers, he mistook their wearied postures as a sign of failure. Then spotting him, the men raised their ice-axes, and pointed toward the summit. As they did so, Hunt realized the wonderful truth. "Far from failure," he wrote later, "this was IT. They had made it!"

Victory on Everest was the result of many things: the fine equipment, from sleeping-bags to oxygen systems; the invaluable information about the route provided by the earlier expeditions; the tireless work of the Sherpa porters; the brilliant leadership of John Hunt; and finally, the courage, determination, and teamwork of the

The south summit, the last obstacle for Hillary and Tenzing. It took them 2½ hours to climb the last 400 feet from there to the summit of Everest.

147

climbers themselves. Reaching the top was a magnificent achievement in itself, but it was all the greater for being accomplished without loss of life or limb. For all these reasons, the first ascent of Everest remains unparalleled in the history of mountaineering.

Just 34 days after the British conquest of Everest, another historic Himalayan ascent took place on Nanga Parbat (26,660 feet). Victory over this, "the killer mountain," was of particular importance to Germany. Of the 31 lives Nanga Parbat had claimed between 1895 and 1950, 26 of them had been lost in the course of German attempts on the peak. There burned in all German climbers a desire to avenge these tragic deaths by mastering the mountain. And, in 1953, a large and highly professional German party set out to do just that. The expedition was led by Dr. Karl Herrligkoffer, the stepbrother of Willy Merkl who had perished in the 1934 assault on the mountain. Among the party was a man named Hermann Buhl, an Austrian mountaineer already well-known for his daring solo climbs.

The assault was launched with methodical care, and it took eight weeks for the party to reach a point below the famous "Silver Saddle" on the ridge leading to the summit. Here, a team of two men was chosen to make the final ascent: Hermann Buhl and Otto Kempter. Their plan was to start off at 3 A.M., but soon after midnight Buhl was up and anxious to be off. There was an argument, and Buhl set off alone. Kempter attempted to catch up with him later, but soon gave up, exhausted. Meanwhile, Buhl was making rapid progress high above the saddle on the crystalline surface of the steep east face of the mountain. Noon came and went, and still he climbed, driving himself forward hour after hour. He reached the summit at 7 P.M., almost at the end of his strength. Nevertheless, he forced himself to take photographs as proof of his triumph before starting back down in the direction of the camp. But already the sun was going down, and Buhl had to seek shelter on the mountainside—without tent or sleeping-bag—in sub-zero weather. Miraculously, he not only survived that terrible night in the open, but managed, still completely alone, to make his way down to the camp the following day. He was severely frostbitten and almost dead from exhaustion, but he had conquered Nanga Parbat—and done it *alone*.

The year 1953 was to witness yet another feat of human daring and endurance—but it was a feat of a very different kind from Buhl's. This time, the objective was Mount Godwin Austen—at

Above: Hermann Buhl after his solo climb to Nanga Parbat's summit, his face showing the exhaustion and strain of his solitary climb. He had been scheduled to climb with Otto Kempter, but they had a disagreement about the time to start, and Buhl went on alone.

Left: Tensing Norgay stands truimphant, 29,028 feet above sea level, on the top of Mount Everest, photographed by Edmund Hillary. They reached the top at 11:30 A.M. on May 29, 1953.

Right: Nanga Parbat, the dreaded killer mountain, which was finally conquered by the 1953 expedition led by Dr. Karl Herrligkoffer. Hermann Buhl, climbing alone, succeeded in reaching the top.

28,250 feet, the world's second highest mountain. First attempted in 1909 by the Duke of the Abruzzi, it had been the subject of two assaults in the 1930's, both of them by Americans. The first, in 1938, under the leadership of Dr. Charles Houston, had made a careful reconnaisance of the Abruzzi Ridge and confirmed the practicality of this southeast route to the summit. The entire expedition had been well-planned and carried out with care.

The second American venture, which took place a year later, in 1939, was badly organized and ended in disaster. High on the Abruzzi Ridge, one of the climbers, Dudley Wolfe, fell seriously ill. Believing that a party from lower down the ridge was on its way up and would look after the ailing man, the ascent leader, Fritz Wiessner, and one Sherpa, left him in the high camp and continued with the climb. But as a result of a misunderstanding, no one did come up from the lower camp, and the sick man remained alone for more than a week. By the time the mistake was realized, no member of the party was fit enough to attempt a rescue. The brave Sherpa Pasang Kikuli—a veteran of many a Himalayan climb, including Nanga Parbat and Nanda Devi—volunteered to bring Wolfe down. But the attempt ended in tragedy. Pasang Kikuli and two other Sherpas died with Wolfe in a blizzard high up on the mountain.

In 1953, Dr. Houston led another assault on Godwin Austen with six Americans, Robert Bates, George Bell, Robert Craig, Arthur Gilkey, Dee Molenaar, and Peter Schoening, and an English climber, Tony Streather. The ascent up the steep rise of the Abruzzi Ridge took the party almost two months of hard climbing, and they

Above: a climber negotiates a very difficult wall of sheer ice—ignoring the breathtaking view—on Godwin Austen. He was a member of the 1938 team led by Charles Houston. Below: in 1953 Houston again led an assault on Godwin Austen. Here he crosses a rope bridge with some of the porters on the way to the expedition base camp.

had reached only 25,500 feet when they were struck by a week-long storm. When the weather finally improved, young Gilkey was found to be suffering from thrombo-phlebitis. He had a blood-clot in his leg and could not walk. He had to be brought down the mountain somehow, and as quickly as possible, if his life were to be saved. The other men improvised a stretcher for him and began the extremely hazardous task of lowering the helpless man down the sheer, ice-encrusted wall of the ridge. Gilkey weighed 185 pounds, and it took the efforts of all seven of the other men to manoeuver the stretcher on which he lay. Two went ahead to find the route; two held the projecting ends of the stretcher; two more pulled back on the ropes from which the stretcher was suspended; and one served as a relay to pass on the shouted messages of the pathfinders below to the men steering and holding the stretcher above.

The going became slower and more difficult as the day wore on. The weather worsened, the slope became ever more perilously steep, and the men grew terribly weary. Suddenly, Bell slipped and fell, dragging Streather, to whom he was roped, with him. As they hurtled downward, their rope tangled with the one connecting Houston and Bates, who were torn off the mountain after their

Above: Camp VIII, 25,500 feet up on Godwin Austen, where the team was trapped for 7 days by a storm.
Below: Charles S. Houston, who was the leader of the ill-starred 1953 attempt to conquer Godwin Austen.

companions. In turn, Bates and Houston's rope tangled with the one linking Molenaar to Gilkey and Schoening. Molenaar, too, was dragged down, but Schoening, who had driven his ax deep into the ice-wall, was not. Miraculously, his ax held, and so did the rope which attached it to him and Gilkey. The lives of five men depended on Schoening, and somehow, he was able to hang on until the others—dazed and injured, but alive—could work their way back onto the face. They managed to lash Gilkey to the mountainside, and then stationed themselves on a ledge a few hundred feet away to wait for morning. When dawn came, they discovered to their horror that Gilkey had been swept away by an avalanche during the night. Racked with exhaustion, and in great pain from the injuries they had suffered in the fall, the seven survivors somehow made their way down the mountain. They had not succeeded in conquering Mount Godwin Austen, but they had willingly risked their lives—and almost lost them—to save a dying companion.

The following year, the peak was scaled by an Italian party under the leadership of Ardito Desio. Again the ascent was made up the Abruzzi Ridge, again the ascent was a long and hazardous one, and again a man lost his life. One of the climbers, Mario Puchoz, died of pneumonia before he could be brought down to safety.

The year 1955 saw the ascent of yet another of the Himalayan giants that had defied previous attempts. This was Kanchenjunga (28,168 feet), third among the world's highest mountains after Everest and Godwin Austen. Situated on the Sikkim-Nepal border, Kanchenjunga is another of the Himalayan peaks deemed sacred by the people of the highlands, and its name means "The Five Treasures of the Snow." But from the mountaineer's point of view, Kanchenjunga's name might more appropriately be rendered as "The Five Terrors of the Snow," for its most notorious characteristics are its frequent blizzards and avalanches, and its perilous glaciers, icefalls, and séracs. These factors make Kanchenjunga one of the hardest of all the Himalayan peaks to climb. Before the 1955 assault, no fewer than seven expeditions were defeated by the mountain. The two most notable of these attempts were made by German teams in 1929 and 1931. Both were led by the brilliant climber Paul Bauer and both were carried out in the teeth of the worst conditions Kanchenjunga can offer: howling blizzards, incessant avalanches, and diabolically shifting snow surfaces. These savage conditions, despite the heroic, almost superhuman efforts made by Bauer and his teammates, defeated both expeditions a few thousand feet below the summit.

When, under the leadership of Charles Evans, a British expedition set off to conquer Kanchenjunga in 1955, it went armed with the most advanced of modern climbing equipment: aerial reconnaissance photographs of the mountain; radio-relay systems; and three kinds of oxygen apparatus (open-circuit, closed-circuit and a type for use during sleep). This equipment—and the high degree of skill and determination displayed by the team members—enabled

Left: members of the 1955 British expedition to Kanchenjunga, which approached within a few feet of the summit, and then descended. The actual topmost point was left untouched as Charles Evans, the expedition leader, had promised the ruler of Sikkim. The people of Sikkim hold the mountain to be the dwelling place of a deity.

Above: Makalu I (27,824 feet), a near neighbor of Mount Everest. Makalu was first climbed in 1955 by the French.

the party to ascend the difficult lower slopes of the mountain in record time. Nevertheless, the climb from the Yalung Glacier, at the base of the southwest face, to the giant snowfield called the Great Shelf, took them more than six weeks.

Just above the Great Shelf, at a height of about 26,000 feet, they established their last camp. From here, on the morning of May 25, the final ascent pair set off for the summit. They were George Band, who, like Charles Evans, had been in the 1953 Everest expedition, and Joe Brown, the finest ice- and rock-climber of his generation. He and Evans needed all their skill and experience to traverse the difficult approach that brought them at last to within a few feet of the summit. And here they stopped and went back down. Why, after so many weeks of effort, did they turn their backs on the summit when it was within their reach? The answer lies in a promise given by Charles Evans to the ruler of Sikkim before the expedition set out. Knowing that the people of Sikkim believed the summit of the mountain to be the dwelling-place of a deity, Evans gave his word that neither he nor any of his party would desecrate the sanctuary. Thus, despite the men's success in overcoming Kanchenjunga's many challenges, they left the mountain without ever having reached its topmost point. Bare of either footsteps, flags, or other symbols of human conquest, Kanchenjunga's summit remained as virgin after their ascent as it had been since it first reared its glittering head, thousands of years ago.

But such was not the case with 13 others of the Himalayan giants. Already, five of their summits had borne—for however brief a time— the imprint of a climber's crampons. These five were Annapurna,

Left: the treacherous lower reaches of the Khumbu Glacier. During the United States expedition in 1963, one of the climbers, John Breitenbach, was killed in the Khumbu Icefall.

Everest, Nanga Parbat, Godwin Austen, and Cho Oyu (26,867 feet), which was conquered by an Austrian team in 1954. Makalu I (27,824 feet), near neighbor of Everest, was climbed by a French party in 1955. In 1956 there were three first ascents of peaks over 26,000 feet high: Manaslu (26,658 feet), by a Japanese team; Gasherbrum II (26,450 feet), by an Austrian team; and Lhotse I (27,890 feet), by a Swiss team. The Swiss expedition, led by Albert Eggler, followed up their triumph on Lhotse (until then the highest unscaled peak in the world) by making *two* ascents of Everest via the South Col the same season. In 1957, Broad Peak (26,414 feet) was climbed by an Austrian party that included Hermann Buhl, the conqueror of Nanga Parbat, and Gasherbrum I (26,470 feet) was

Above: Jim Whittaker and Nawang Gombu, two of the six men that the American expedition in 1963 put on the summit of Everest. The most spectacular result of the expedition was the first-ever Himalayan traverse, when Thomas Hornbein and William Unsoeld climbed the summit by way of the west ridge and descended by the South Col route.

scaled by an American team under the leadership of Nicholas Clinch. A Swiss team mastered Annapurna's near neighbor, Dhaulagiri (26,810 feet) in 1960. The lowliest of the mighty 14, Gosainthan (26,291 feet) was conquered in 1964.

When all 14 of the greatest Himalayan peaks, as well as many of the lesser ones, had been scaled, the search for fresh challenges led inevitably to the forging of new routes. Two of the most exciting of these "new route" ascents were the American conquest of Everest by the west ridge in 1963, and the British conquest of Annapurna by the south face in 1970.

The American objective in the 1963 assault on Everest was nothing less than the traverse of the highest point on earth. The plan was to ascend by the west ridge—a first in itself—and then to descend by way of the traditional South Col route. The party, led by Norman G. Dyhrenfurth, was some 20 men strong, and it required the concerted efforts of the whole team to establish the series of camps along the ridge from which the traverse was to be made.

Tragedy struck early in the assault, when young John Breitenbach was killed by a huge block of falling ice in the Khumbu Icefall. Tragedy almost struck again two months later at 25,500 feet, when the final ascent pair, Thomas F. Hornbein and William F. Unsoeld, with the members of the support team, were camped on a ledge of snow jutting out from the west ridge. In the middle of the night a fierce wind blew up. The gale tugged and pulled at the tents, and at last tore them from their moorings. The tents—with six men still inside—were blown to the very brink of the ice-ledge where, by a miracle, they were stopped by a trough of snow.

Safe, but severely shaken, the party was forced to descend to the camp below. But three days later they were back once more, high on the west ridge. From a camp at 27,250 feet, Hornbein and Unsoeld set out for the summit at 6:30 A.M. on May 22. Twelve hours of unceasing effort in a fiercely cold wind brought them to the top of Everest. There to greet them was the American flag planted by two other members of the expedition—James W. Whittaker and the Sherpa Nawang Gombu—who had reached the summit by the South Col route three weeks before. The same flag, a bit frayed, but still flying bravely, had greeted two other climbers, Luther G. Jerstad and Barry C. Bishop, a mere three hours before Hornbein and Unsoeld reached the top. Like Whittaker and Gombu, Jerstad and Bishop had made the ascent by the South Col route. They were now on their way down, and Unsoeld and Hornbein were able to follow their footsteps for a time.

For the west ridgers, of course, the return by the South Col route was a journey into the unknown. Again and again they lost the tracks they were following and, as darkness closed in, the two men found themselves floundering in a feathery gray world, unsure of their direction. They began to call for help, hoping that they would be heard by members of the support team from Camp VI. At last, miraculously, they heard answering shouts from below. For two

hours, guided by these shouts, they toiled downward in the dark. When they reached the two dim figures waiting for them below, they were astonished to discover that they were Jerstad and Bishop!

All four climbers were by now exhausted and their oxygen supply was dangerously low. Still they pressed on, hour after hour, until they could go no farther. At 12:30 A.M. they found a level place in the ridge and settled down to wait for morning. They had no tent, no sleeping-bags, no food or drink—and no more oxygen. The temperature was −18°F. and they were still above 28,000 feet. Never before had any man remained in the open at that height and

The south face of Annapurna, among the most formidable rock faces in the world, culminating in a wall of ice and rock 12,000 feet high. It was this which the 1970 British expedition, led by Chris Bonington, set out to conquer.

lived to tell the tale. And, had the usual fierce Everest wind been blowing, they would certainly have perished. But luck was with them. The wind died away, and at dawn, after a calm, starlit night, the four men found themselves still alive and still able to move. Two hours after they began to stumble downward again, they were found by the support team and taken to the camp below.

Few expeditions have achieved such a spectacular series of triumphs as did the American Everest team of 1963. Not only did the team accomplish the first west ridge ascent and the first traverse of Everest, but it also managed to put no less than six climbers on the summit, four of whom broke all previous records by surviving a night in the open, without camping gear or oxygen, at 28,000 feet.

The goal of the 1970 British expedition to Annapurna was to

Dougal Haston and Don Whillans on Annapurna. While they were searching for a suitable camp site for the highest camp, the weather suddenly cleared, revealing the summit. They decided to try for the top, although they were unroped and not equipped with oxygen.

achieve the first conquest of the peak by the sheer south face. Led by Chris Bonington, the team consisted of 11 exceptionally skilled climbers. (Tragically, one of them, Ian Clough, was to be killed by a falling ice-pillar at the very end of the expedition.)

The south face of Annapurna is one of the most formidable rock faces in the world. Its final 12,000 feet consists of a wall of ice and rock that soars almost vertically to the summit. The British team, like the American team on Everest, had to battle against severe winds most of the way up. Camp VI was established at 24,000 feet. In the gray dawn on May 21, Don Whillans and Dougal Haston set off to reconnoiter a site for Camp VII. Suddenly the weather cleared, and they could see the summit. It was still early in the morning, and they decided to make a try for it. Unroped, and without oxygen, they slowly inched their way up to the final section—50 feet of almost-vertical rock glazed with ice. This too, they mastered, and stood at last on Annapurna's summit.

Haston and Whillans' ascent of the south face of Annapurna is certain to become a mountaineering legend for several reasons: first, because the decision to attempt the final assault was made on the spur of the moment; second, because they climbed beyond 26,000 feet without the security of rope or oxygen reserves, and third, because the final ascent is one of the hardest in the world.

In 1953, when Everest was climbed, some sections of the non-mountaineering public thought that, with the conquest of the world's highest peak, mountain climbing must grind to a halt. Just how wrong they were was shown in the period of spectacular Himalayan climbs that followed. And now, when many of the great Himalayan peaks have been climbed, mountaineers have begun forging new routes, like those on Everest and Annapurna, and undertaking ever-more awesome feats of daring.

The world still holds a myriad of mountaineering challenges for the ardent climber. Hundreds of peaks—in the Andes and the Himalaya, the Pamirs, and the ranges of Antarctica—remain unscaled. Moreover, thousands of routes—in the oft-climbed Alps, as well as in every other major range—remain unexplored.

Since the Golden Age of the mid-1800's, mountaineering has seen the innovation of numerous new climbing methods and techniques. And there will be many more in the years to come, as mountaineers continue to seek out ever greater challenges to their endurance and their ingenuity. For once conceived, the mountaineer's need to climb becomes as impossible to deny as it is to explain. To go on finding the challenge, satisfaction, and inspiration he has once discovered in mountain climbing, he will continue to assail the heights by whatever combination of routes, techniques, and conditions suits him best. He is drawn to climb mountains by something which he may call a love of adventure or a wish to explore, the search for relaxation or the desire for conquest. But in every true mountaineer, the final, compelling reason for climbing is simply his deep and abiding love for the mountains themselves.

A Victorian mountaineer works his way across a rock outcropping—a drawing by Edward Whymper that captures the continuing fascination of climbing.

Appendix

Left: the 1970 Annapurna expedition was an example of modern mountaineering—showing that even after the highest peaks have been conquered, there are challenges remaining to the dedicated mountaineer. Here Chris Bonington works his way slowly up Annapurna's south face, pioneering a new route.

After two centuries of exploration and conquest, the world's mountains have lost much of their mystery, but none of their peril. Unlike most of the earth's remaining wildernesses, they cannot be "civilized," but remain—no matter how often they are climbed—as untamed and dangerous as they are beautiful. It is this fact which makes mountaineering as much an experience of high adventure for the modern climber as it was for the early alpinists. And it is the feeling of adventure—of imminent peril, supreme challenge, and heady exhilaration—which makes mountaineers' own reports of their climbs so riveting.

The first part of this appendix offers an exciting glimpse into the experience of climbing as it is seen and felt by mountaineers themselves. Here, in the dramatic contrast between a medieval report of a mountain dragon and Maurice Herzog's account of the conquest of Annapurna, the evolution in man's attitude toward mountains can be clearly seen. Here also, in such records as Rébuffat's joyful description of guiding, Whymper's drawings of the Matterhorn, and Tenzing's tribute to Everest, is found the real essence of the climber's passion for mountains.

Following this selection of mountaineering documents is a brief biographical dictionary of the most important climbers mentioned in the text. Each entry lists the mountaineer's most significant achievements, and is accompanied by a photograph of the climber.

Immediately after the biography section is a table which gives pertinent information about 56 of the world's most famous mountains, and a glossary which explains and amplifies the meaning of the specialized mountaineering terms and phrases used in the text.

An index and a list of picture credits for *Roof of the World* completes this appendix.

Mountain Dragons

During the Middle Ages—and, in fact, well into the 1700's—mountains were believed to be haunted by all kinds of ferocious demons and dragons. The creatures described in the following two excerpts are typical of the sort of beasts once thought to dwell in the heights. In the first passage, a medieval monk named Fra Salimbene describes what befell King Peter of Aragon when he tried to scale a Pyrenean peak in the 1200's. In the second, a traveler named Christopher Schorer (writing some four centuries later) describes an almost identical experience, this time in the Alps.

"On the borders of Provence and Spain there rises a very high mountain which the inhabitants of the neighborhood call Canigosus. . . . On that mountain no man has ever lived, nor has any son of man ever dared to ascend it. . . .

"When Peter of Arragon had decided to make the ascent of that mountain, wishing to make the experiment and ascertain what there was on the top of it, he called two knights, his intimate friends, to whom he was much attached, and explained to them what he proposed to do. They rejoiced, and promised, not only that they would keep his project secret, but also that they would never desert him. Taking provisions, therefore, and the weapons that seemed appropriate, and leaving their horses at the foot of the mountain where there are inhabitants, they began slowly to make the ascent on foot. When they had ascended a considerable distance they began to hear very horrible and terrible thunder claps; in addition to this, flashes of lightning began to appear and storms of hail to fall: All which things so terrified them that they threw themselves upon the ground, and lay there, as it were, lifeless, in their fear and apprehension of the calamities which had overtaken them.

"Peter, who was stronger and more courageous than the others, bade them wait for him until the evening of the following day, and then, if he should not return, to descend from the mountain, and depart withersoever they would. So Peter, with great labor, made the ascent alone; and when he was on the top of the mountain he found a lake there; and when he threw a stone into the lake, a horrible dragon of enormous size came out of it, and began to fly about in the air, and to darken the air with its breath. After this, Peter descended to his companions, and reported, unfolded, and

Above: it was believed that dragons lurking in the mountain heights dropped "dragonstones," which were supposed to have magical healing powers. This dragon, from a map by Scheuchzer, is flying out of the mountain, having produced two of the dragonstones.

Above right: the stories of dragons in the Alps might have been encouraged by glimpses from a distance, through the mountain storms, of a serpent-like glacier twisting down the high valleys.

Left: a dragon reportedly seen in 1660 from Scheuchzer's description of the natural history of the Alpine region.

narrated to them, everything that he had seen and done; and as they were on their way down from the mountain, he instructed them to tell the whole story to whomsoever they chose."

"In the year 1649, I was contemplating the beauty of the heavens by night, when lo! and behold, I saw a bright and shining dragon issue from a large cave in the mountain commonly called Pilatus, and fly about, swiftly flapping its wings. It was very large; its tail was long; its neck extended; its head terminated in the serrated jaw of a serpent. While it was flying, it threw out sparks, just as the red-hot horseshoe does when hammered by the blacksmith. My first impression was that I saw a meteor, but after careful observation, I recognized that it was a dragon, from the nature of its movements and the structure of its various limbs."

The Early Mountaineers, *Francis Gribble (T. Fisher Unwin: London, 1899) pp.* 15–16, 80–81.

The Role of the Guide

The help and companionship of professional guides has been an integral part of mountaineering since the great days of the Golden Age. Despite the advent of "guideless climbing," skilled guides are still in great demand in the Alps. Gaston Rébuffat, a French climber who took part in the 1950 Annapurna expedition, is a professional guide. In this passage, he describes the joys and dangers of his work.

"The profession of guide helped me to become a man; it is among the finest that exist, for it is practiced in the unspoilt regions of the earth's surface.

"In this modern age, very little remains that is real. Night has been banished, so have the cold, the wind, and the stars. . . . What a strange encounter then is that between man and the high places of his planet! Up there he is surrounded by the silence of forgetfulness. If there is a slope of snow steep as a glass window, he climbs it . . . if there is a rock perfect as an obelisk, he defies gravity and proves that he can get up anywhere.

"Guides are no foolhardy adventurers: they live, they do their job. Every day in the summer they get up very early to question the sky and the wind. The day before, perhaps, they were uneasy, for long clouds scarred the western horizon. They feared a night of worsening weather; the Milky Way shone too brightly, the cold delayed its coming. But now, if the north wind has won the upper hand, the weather is good, the guide can rouse his client and set out. Then the rope will join together two beings who now live as one. During these hours the guide is linked with a stranger who will become a friend. When two men share the good and the bad, then they are no longer strangers.

"This profession might become wearisome through the repetition of the same climbs time after time, but the guide is more than a mere machine for climbing rocks and ice slopes, for knowing the weather and the way. He does not climb for himself, he throws open the gates of his mountains as a gardener opens the gates of his garden. The heights are a splendid setting for his work, and climbing gives him a pleasure of which he never tires. But above all he is repaid by the pleasure of the man he guides. He knows that such-and-such a climb is particularly interesting, that at this turn the view is quite suddenly very beautiful, and that this ice ridge is delicate as lace.

Above: Cachat, the guide who was known as "the Giant." He climbed Mont Blanc with De Saussure, and accompanied him on the later expedition with his son.

Below: climbers often chose to climb with the same guide year after year. Melchior Anderegg (left) was not only the favorite guide of Charles Matthews, here with him, but of Leslie Stephen.

He says nothing of all this, but his reward is in his companion's smile of discovery. If the guide thought to win his pleasure only from his own climbing, he would be robbed of it and soon tire of the mountains. In fact, though he may climb the same crack or the same slope five, ten, or twenty times a summer, he rejoices each time to renew acquaintance. But his real happiness derives from a deeper pleasure, that of his kinship with the mountains and the elements, just as the peasant is akin to the soil or the workman to the materials with which he works. If the second man on the rope hesitates, the guide restores his confidence. If the storm breaks suddenly, he knows its secrets, his instinct masters it, his sense of responsibility multiplies his strength tenfold, and he brings his party back safe to the hut. He loves difficulty but abhors danger, which is a very different thing. Sometimes, it is true, he is killed by lightning, stone-fall, or avalanche. That too is part of the job; but so long as he lives he strives to lead his rope safely."

Starlight and Storm, *Gaston Rébuffat, trans. by Wilfrid Noyce and Sir John Hunt (J. M. Dent and Sons: London, 1956) pp. xvi–xviii.*

Below: this sort of expedition—here a party climbing on a glacier in the Mont Blanc region in the 1860's—had to rely heavily on the guides for their experience and skill in the mountains.

A Storm on the Matterhorn

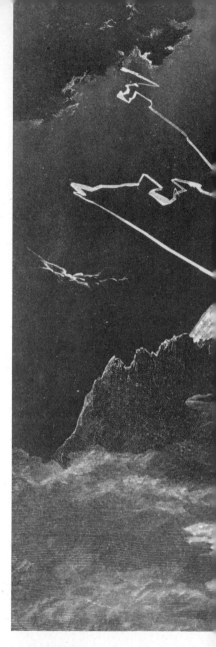

A severe storm in the heights is one of the most spectacular dangers a climber can encounter in the Alps. In the following passage, Edward Whymper describes the storm which overtook himself and Jean-Antoine Carrel during their joint assault on the Matterhorn in 1863.

"We went on gaily, passed the second tent platform, the Chimney, and the other well-remembered points, and reckoned, confidently, on sleeping that night upon the top of the 'the shoulder'; but, before we had well arrived at the foot of the Great Tower, a sudden rush of cold air warned us to look out.

"It was difficult to say where this air came from; it did not blow as a wind, but descended rather as the water in a shower-bath! All was tranquil again; the atmosphere *showed* no signs of disturbance; there was a dead calm, and not a speck of cloud to be seen anywhere. But we did not remain very long in this state. The cold air came again, and this time it was difficult to say where it did *not* come from. We jammed down our hats as it beat against the ridge and screamed amongst the crags. Before we had got to the foot of the Tower, mists had been formed above and below. They appeared at first in small, isolated patches (in several places at the same time), which danced and jerked and were torn into shreds by the wind, but grew larger under the process. They were united together, and rent again— showing us the blue sky for a moment, and blotting it out the next; and augmented incessantly, until the whole heavens were filled with whirling, boiling clouds. Before we could take off our packs, and get under any kind of shelter, a hurricane of snow burst upon us from the east. It fell very heavily, and in a few minutes the ridge was covered by it 'What shall we do?' I shouted to Carrel. 'Monsieur,' said he, the wind is bad; the weather has changed; we are heavily laden. Here is a fine gîte [resting place]; let us stop. If we go on we shall be half-frozen. That is *my* opinion.' No one differed from him; so we fell to work to make a place for the tent and in a couple of hours had completed the platform. . . . The clouds had blackened during that time, and we had hardly finished our task before a thunderstorm broke upon us with appalling fury. Forked lightning shot out at the turrets above, and at the crags below. It was so close that we quailed at its darts. It seemed to scorch us—we were in the very focus of the storm. The thunder was simultaneous with the

Left: a drawing by Whymper showing The Crags of the Matterhorn in a storm during an early attempt on the Italian Ridge. His tent was pitched below the Great Tower (shown at center right).

Below left: Edward Whymper's drawings made a great contribution to the development of mountaineering, even when it was claimed they were exaggerated.

Right: Whymper, in 1862, crouching under a rock to escape a cannonade of stones "of at least a foot cube" in a small rock avalanche on the Matterhorn.

flashes; short and sharp, and more like the noise of a door that is violently slammed, multiplied a thousandfold, than any noise to which I can compare it. . . .

"The wind during all this time seemed to blow tolerably consistently from the east. It smote the tent so vehemently (notwithstanding it was partly protected by rocks) that we had grave fears our refuge might be blown away bodily, with ourselves inside. . . . There was little chance of sleeping, between the noise of the wind, of the thunder, and of the falling rocks. I forgave the thunder for the sake of the lightning. A more splendid spectacle than its illumination of the Matterhorn crags I do not expect to see."

Scrambles Amongst the Alps in the Years 1860–69, *Edward Whymper* (*John Murray: London,* 1871) *pp.* 171–172, 174–175.

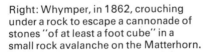

Waiting for Rescue

What is it like to fall into a crevasse while climbing alone, and then to wait for days, hoping against all hope that someone will find you? Georges Sonnier describes such an experience here.

"I think of this other solitary climber, who, when coming back from an expedition on the Aletch Glacier, broke through a snow-bridge and fell into a crevasse. The hole was bottomless. By great luck, he fell on a snow-bridge some twenty feet below the surface and was only slightly injured.

"He was alive. Alive, but alone, abandoned, lost at the bottom of an ice hole, above which he saw but a narrow stretch of blue sky and, at night, a few faint twinkling stars.

Above: Ulrich Almer, on the Gabelhorn in 1880, holding his three companions who fell 2,000 feet when a snow cornice collapsed. Almer leaped backward from the crack and plunged his ax into the snow, which caught and held the party.

Left: a large crevasse, and the method which Whymper and his guides would have used to cross it. This sort of crevasse is found as a climber moves up past the glacier to the rocks above.

"He was there for eight days and seven nights, eating only a little chocolate which he melted over the flame of a candle and diluted with the glacier water that dripped over him. With this tiny flame he also tried to thaw his hands and feet, slowly becoming frozen by the endless night of the glacier depths.

"Eight days and seven nights! No search party had found anything. Everybody thought he was dead, even his friends. . . . For living people, this living man was but a name and a shadow.

"And yet, obstinately, he persisted in living. His ice-ax had become stuck in the broken snow-bridge. With a frightful exertion he managed to climb up to within one meter [about 40 inches] of it; a single meter from light, freedom, warmth and life. But that one last meter was beyond him . . . he fell back.

"He tried again seven times, and always in vain. Clutching at the ice with his bleeding hands, which were now without sensation, he crept up the terrible, steel-colored wall, and finally dropped back into the night of his ice prison. He was exhausted and had to abandon his attempts. Then, on the evening of the fourth day, the ice-ax fell beside him. It was useless now, for he no longer had the strength to use it.

"Sometimes he heard parties passing above him. He heard words, songs, laughter, and he shouted in vain. The edges of the crevasse were formed in such a way that they magnified the sounds that came from outside, while shutting in those which might come from below. So the prisoner's voice was captive too. . . .

"I can picture to myself the wounded man, fighting against so much cruelty, against the exquisite torture of the mountain; abandoned by everything, left at the gate of the next world and yet fighting, still fighting in the shadows. . . . There is no word to describe such courage. . . .

"And yet he was saved at last by a miracle—a lesser miracle than that of his dogged protracted fight. Passing near the crevasse, a guide noticed the broken bridge, drew near and saw the prisoner. That very night he was brought down to the valley, half his body frozen and his burnt eyes full of shadow."

Excerpt from Où règne la lumière, *by Georges Sonnier, translated in* Mont Blanc: An Anthology, *by Claire Eliane Engel (George Allen and Unwin: London, 1965) pp. 168–169.*

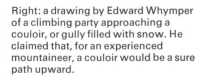

Right: a drawing by Edward Whymper of a climbing party approaching a couloir, or gully filled with snow. He claimed that, for an experienced mountaineer, a couloir would be a sure path upward.

The Moment of Conquest

The final moments of any climb are ones of tremendous excitement and exhilaration. But perhaps this was never more true than in the last stages of the ascent of Annapurna in 1950. In this extract Maurice Herzog describes his feelings as he and Louis Lachenal approached the summit of this mighty peak.

"Even through dark glasses the snow was blinding and the sun beat straight on the ice. We looked down upon precipitous ridges which dropped away into space, and upon tiny glaciers far, far below. . . . Suddenly Lachenal grabbed me:

" 'If I go back, what will you do?'

"A whole sequence of pictures flashed through my head: the days of marching in sweltering heat, the hard pitches we had overcome, the tremendous efforts we had all made to lay siege to the mountain, the daily heroism of all my friends in establishing the camps. . . . Today we were consecrating an ideal, and no sacrifice was too great. My voice rang out clearly:

" 'I should go on by myself. . . .'

"The die was cast. . . . Nothing could stop us now from getting to the top. The psychological atmosphere changed with these few words, and we went forward now as brothers. . . .

"The snow, sprinkled over every rock and gleaming in the sun, was of a radiant beauty that touched me to the heart. I had never seen such complete transparency; I was living in a world of crystal. Sounds were indistinct, the atmosphere like cotton wool.

"An astonishing happiness welled up in me, but I could not define it. Everything was so new, so utterly unprecedented. It was not in the least like anything I had known in the Alps. . .This was a different universe—withered, desert, lifeless; a fantastic universe where the presence of man was not foreseen, perhaps not desired. We were braving an interdict, overstepping a boundary, and yet we had no fear as we continued upwards. . . .

" 'Couloir!'

"A finger pointed. The whispered word from one to another indicated the key to the rocks—the last line of defense. . .It was fairly steep, and we had a minute's hesitation. Should we have enough strength left to overcome this final obstacle?

"Fortunately the snow was hard, and by kicking steps we were able to manage, thanks to our crampons. A false move would have

Above: Don Whillans on the summit of Annapurna, after the remarkable ascent by the south face route in 1970. The picture is a still from the movie film taken by Dougal Haston on the climb.

Above right: the Japanese team on the summit of the Eiger, triumphant after their ascent by the direct route. The Japanese have achieved many spectacular successes in mountaineering during the last few years, with their climbers active in the Alps and the Himalaya.

Left: a party rests on the summit of Mont Blanc in 1838. The challenge of reaching the very top remains the lure for the most experienced mountaineers today, although the problem has changed from the simple matter of getting there, to the more complex one of finding the most demanding route.

been fatal. There was no need to make handholds—our axes, driven in as far as possible, served us for an anchor. . . .

"But where was the top—left or right? Stopping at every breath, leaning on our axes, we tried to recover our breath and to calm down our hearts, which were thumping as though they would burst. . . . No need to exchange looks— each of us would have read the same determination in the other's eyes. A slight detour to the left, a few more steps—the summit ridge came gradually nearer—a few rocks to avoid. We dragged ourselves up. Could we possibly be there?

"Yes!

"A fierce and savage wind tore at us.

"We were on top of Annapurna! 8,075 meters, 26,493 feet.

"Our hearts overflowed with an unspeakable happiness.

" 'If only the others could know. . . .

"If only everyone could know!"

Annapurna, *Maurice Herzog, trans. by Nea Morin and Janet Adam Smith (The Reprint Society: London,* 1954) *pp.* 190–193.

Everest . . . Who Got There First?

After the conquest of Everest in 1953, there was an insistent demand to know which man—the New Zealander Edmund Hillary or the Sherpa Tenzing Norgay—had been the first to reach the summit. Here Tenzing answers the question.

"I have thought much about what I will say now—of how Hillary and I reached the summit of Everest. Later, when we came down from the mountain, there was much foolish talk about who got there first. Some said it was I, some Hillary. Some that only one of us got there—or neither. . . . And in Kathmandu, to put a stop to such talk, Hillary and I signed a statement in which we said 'We reached the summit almost together.' We hoped this would be the end of it. But it was not the end. . . . And all over the world I am asked, 'Who got there first? Who got there first?'

"Again I say, 'It is a foolish question. The answer means nothing.' And yet it is a question that has been asked so often . . . that I feel, after long thought, that the answer should be given. As will be clear, it is not for my own sake that I give it. Nor is it for Hillary's. It is for the sake of Everest. . . .

Above: Tenzing, who made the final leg of the climb with Hillary to bring success to the 1953 British Everest Expedition. He was 39, and had been on Everest expeditions since 1935.

Above: some of the materials and porters necessary for the British to put two men in a position to reach the summit of Everest. The expedition, led by John Hunt, had 14 climbers in all.

"A little below the summit Hillary and I stopped. We looked up. Then we went on. The rope that joined us was thirty feet long, but I held most of it in loops in my hand, so that there was only about six feet between us. I was not thinking of 'first' and 'second.' I did not say to myself, 'There is a golden apple up there. I will push Hillary aside and run for it.' We went on slowly, steadily. And then we were there. Hillary stepped on top first. And I stepped up after him.

"If, after all the talk and argument, the answer seems quiet and simple, I can only say that that is as it should be. Many of my own people, I know, will be disappointed at it. They have given a great and false importance to the idea that it must be I who was 'first.' These people have been good and wonderful to me, and I owe them much. But I owe more to Everest—and to the truth. . . . Over and over again I have asked myself, 'What will future generations think of us if we allow the facts of our achievement to stay shrouded in mystery? Will they not feel ashamed of us—two comrades in life and death—who have something to hide from the world?' And each time I asked it the answer was the same: 'Only the truth is good enough for the future. Only the truth is good enough for Everest.'"

Left: Tenzing and Hillary (right) back at camp after the successful ascent to the top of the world's highest mountain. The triumphant news reached London on the day Elizabeth II was crowned.

Man of Everest: The Autobiography of Tenzing *as told to James Ramsey Ullman (George G. Harrap: London,* 1955*) pp.* 267–269.

The Mountaineers

ABRUZZI

Abruzzi, Luigi Amadeo, Duke of the (1873–1933). Italian mountaineer-explorer. A pioneer of winter climbing in the Alps. Organized and led three major mountaineering expeditions: to Alaska in 1897, where he made the first ascent of Mount Saint Elias; to Uganda in 1906, where he explored the Ruwenzori range; and to the Karakoram range in 1909, where he explored the approaches to Godwin Austen and set a height record by climbing to 24,600 feet on Bride Peak.

Almer, Christian (1826–1873). One of the best known Swiss guides of the Golden Age. Took part in Alfred Wills' famous ascent of the Wetterhorn in 1854. Worked with such climbers as Sir Leslie Stephen, Edward Whymper, William Coolidge, and Marguerite Brevoort. Made many first ascents of Alpine peaks. Among these were the Eiger, the west peak of the Grandes Jorasses, and the first winter ascents of the Wetterhorn, the Schreckhorn, and the Jungfrau.

ALMER

Anderegg, Melchior (1827–1914). Noted Swiss guide of the Golden Age. Climbed with such mountaineers as Charles Matthews, Edward Whymper, Sir Leslie Stephen, and Lucy Walker. Among his many first ascents were those of the Zinal Rothhorn, the Dent d'Hérens, and Mont Blanc by the Brenva Ridge.

ANDEREGG

BALMAT

BAUER

BENUZZI

BONATTI

Balmat, Jacques (1762–1834). French peasant who made the first ascent of Mont Blanc with Dr. Paccard in 1786. Served as a guide on De Saussure's ascent of Mont Blanc and the Col du Géant in 1787.

Bauer, Paul (born 1896). German mountaineer. Headed Kanchenjunga expeditions in 1929 and 1931. Made the first ascent of Siniolchu in the Sikkim Himalaya in 1936. Led the fifth German expedition to Nanga Parbat in 1938.

Benuzzi, Felice (born 1910). Italian mountaineer. While a British prisoner of war in Kenya in 1943, he escaped with two companions and led them in an expedition to Mount Kenya. Despite the inadequacy of their provisions and equipment, the three succeeded in reaching the summit of Lenana, the third highest peak of the mountain. They then returned to the British camp and gave themselves up.

Bonatti, Walter (born 1930). Italian mountaineer. Made the first solo ascent of the north face of the Matterhorn in 1953, and of the southwest pillar of the Dru in 1956. Took part in the successful Italian assault on Godwin Austen in 1954, and was one of the first two men to reach the summit of Gasherbrum IV in 1958.

Bonington, Christian (born 1934). British mountaineer. Took part in the assault on Annapurna II in 1960. Made the first British ascent of the Eigerwand in 1962. Assisted in the forging of the Harlin *direttissima* on the Eigerwand in 1966. Led the expedition that made the first ascent of Annapurna by the south face in 1970.

Brown, Joe (born 1930). British mountaineer. Considered the most brilliant rock climber of this century. Took part in the first ascent of Kanchenjunga in 1955 and, with George Band, was the first to reach its summit. In 1956, was one of the first two men to reach the summit of the Mustagh Tower in the Karakoram range.

Bruce, Charles Granville (1866–1939). British mountaineer and explorer. Took part in Martin Conway's expedition to the Kara-

BONINGTON

BROWN

BRUCE

BUHL

CARREL

CASSIN

CLOUGH

koram range in 1892. Pioneered the training of Sherpas for Himalayan expeditions. Headed the British Everest expedition of 1922, and took part in the British Everest expedition of 1924.

Buhl, Hermann (1924–1957). Austrian mountaineer. Climbed extensively in the Alps, where he made the ascent of the Eigerwand, the north face of the Grandes Jorasses, and the Watzmann by the difficult "Salzburg" route. In 1953, he achieved the extraordinary feat of conquering Nanga Parbat *alone*. Took part in the expedition to Broad Peak in the Karakoram range in 1957, shortly before he met his death in an accident in the Baltoro mountains of Kashmir.

Carrel, Jean-Antoine (1829–1890). Italian mountaineer and guide. Was Whymper's arch-rival in the race to conquer the Matterhorn. Made several attempts on the peak (one with Whymper, in 1862) before 1865 when, as leader of an Italian party, he reached the summit by way of the Italian ridge, shortly after Whymper had done so. In 1880, accompanied Whymper to the Andes, where the two climbed Cotopaxi and Chimborazo. Collapsed and died in 1890 after leading a Matterhorn party down to safety during a blizzard.

Cassin, Riccardo (born 1909). Italian mountaineer. Made the first direct ascent of the Grandes Jorasses in 1938. Took part in the Italian reconnaissance of Godwin Austen in 1953. Led the expedition that conquered Gasherbrum IV in 1958. Headed a party of six climbers who scaled Mount McKinley by its sheer south face in 1961.

Clough, Ian (1939–1970). British mountaineer. Made many difficult ascents in the Alps, such as those of the North Face of the Eiger and that of Mont Blanc's Central Pillar of Frêney. Took part in the expedition that achieved the first ascent of Annapurna's south face in 1970. Was killed by a falling ice-pillar during the descent of Annapurna's lower slopes.

Conway, Lord (1856–1937). British mountaineer-explorer. Author of *The Alps from End to End,* and of the *Zermatt Pocket Book,* the first guide book of its kind. In 1892, led the first

CONWAY

major expedition to the Karakoram range, where he carried out extensive exploration and climbed Pioneer Peak. In 1898, traveled to the Andes where he made the first ascent of Illimani and the second ascent of Aconcagua.

Coolidge, William Augustus Brevoort (1850–1926). American mountaineer. First traveled to the Alps as a boy of 14 with his aunt, Marguerite Brevoort. With her, began a mountaineering career that spanned 30 years and included no less than 1,700 Alpine expeditions. Assisted Martin Conway in the production of several climbing guidebooks, and became a prominent Alpine historian.

Croz, Michel-Auguste (1830–1865). French guide. Took part in an expedition through the Dauphiné Alps with A. W. Moore in 1864. The following year served as Whymper's chief guide on the famous Matterhorn climb. Was killed, with Douglas Hadow, Lord Francis Douglas, and Charles Hudson on the descent from the summit.

Dent, Thomas Clinton (1850–1912). British mountaineer. A pioneer of the "new route" school of alpinism, he achieved fame by making the first ascent of the Grand Dru in 1878. Climbed extensively in the Caucasus in the 1880's.

Donkin, William Frederick (1845–1888). British mountaineer. Climbed extensively in the Alps and was one of the first to specialize in mountain photography. Traveled to the Caucasus in 1888 and with Henry Fox, was killed trying to climb Koshtantau.

Dyhrenfurth, Norman Gunther (born 1918). American mountaineer. Took part in Bradford Washburn's Alaskan expedition to Mount Saint Agnes in 1938. Became the first American to set foot on Everest when, in 1952, he served as a member of the Swiss expedition to the mountain. In 1963, led the American expedition which achieved the first ascent of Everest by its west ridge and the first traverse of a major Himalayan peak.

Evans, Dr. Charles (born 1918). British mountaineer. Has climbed extensively in the Alps and in the Canadian Rockies. Took part in

DONKIN   DENT

DYHRENFURTH

EVANS

COOLIDGE

CROZ

DE FILIPPI (CENTER)

FITZGERALD

FORBES

FRESHFIELD

the successful British expedition to Everest in 1953. Leader of the British team that conquered Kanchenjunga in 1955.

Filippi, Filippo de (1869–1938). Italian mountaineer and naturalist. Took part in two of Abruzzi's expeditions (to Mount Saint Elias in 1897 and to the Karakoram range in 1909). Served as the official chronicler of the third of Abruzzi's major expeditions (to the Ruwenzori range in 1906). Led a scientific expedition of his own through Kashmir, Baltistan, and Ladakh in 1913.

FitzGerald, Edward A. (1871–1931). British mountaineer. Traveled extensively in the Alps with Martin Conway in 1894. With his guide Mattias Zurbriggen, made the first ascent of Mount Tasman in New Zealand in 1895. Led the expedition which made the first ascents of Aconcagua and·Tupungato in the Andes in 1897.

Forbes, James David (1809–1868). British mountaineer and scientist. Made significant contributions to the theory of glaciers and, in the course of his scientific research, climbed extensively in the Alps. He became the first British mountaineer to scale the Jungfrau in 1841, and the first British climber to conquer a virgin Alpine summit, the Stockhorn, in 1842.

Freshfield, Douglas W. (1845–1934). British mountaineer, explorer, and geographer. Climbed extensively in the Alps, the Pyrenees, and the Caucasus where, with A. W. Moore and C. C. Tucker, he made the first ascents of Kazbek and the east summit of Elbrus. Headed the search party that attempted to determine what had happened to Donkin and Fox on Koshtantau in 1888. Led a reconnaissance expedition to Kanchenjunga in 1899, and, in the course of his reconnaissance, became the first to circumnavigate the mountain.

Harlin, John (1936–1966). American mountaineer. Climbed extensively in the Alps, where he ascended the north face of the Matterhorn in 1956 and the Eigerwand in 1962. Planned and led the first ascent of the Eigerwand by the most direct route (the *direttissima*), but was killed when his rope broke, two-thirds of the way up. The Eigerwand *direttissima* is now known as the John Harlin route.

Haston, Dougal (born 1942), British mountaineer. Has climbed extensively in the Alps, making ascents of the north face of the

HARLIN (LEFT)

HASTON

HERRLIGKOFFER

HERZOG

HILLARY

HOUSTON

HUNT

Matterhorn, and of the Eigerwand. In 1966, took part in the forging of the Harlin route up the Eigerwand, completing the ascent with a German party after John Harlin had fallen to his death. A member of the British expedition to Annapurna in 1970, he was, with Don Whillans, the first to reach its summit by the south face.

Herrligkoffer, Dr. Karl (born 1919). German mountaineer. One of the few survivors of the disastrous 1934 expedition to Nanga Parbat. Led the German expedition to Nanga Parbat in 1953 on which Hermann Buhl reached the summit. Led the expedition which attained the summit of Nanga Parbat by the Rupal Flank in 1970.

Herzog, Maurice (born 1919). French mountaineer. Headed the French expedition which made a reconnaissance of Dhaulagiri and conquered Annapurna in 1950. Herzog himself, was, with Louis Lachenal, the first to reach the summit of this, the first peak over 26,000 feet ever conquered.

Hillary, Sir Edmund Percival (born 1919). New Zealand mountaineer. Began climbing in the New Zealand Alps in 1939. In 1950, climbed five 13,000-foot peaks in the European Alps in five days. Took part in the British reconnaissance expedition to Everest in 1951, and played a vital role in forging the route through the Khumbu Icefall. A member of the British expedition to Everest in 1953, he was, with Tenzing Norgay, the first to reach its summit. In 1954, took part in a reconnaissance expedition to Mount Makalu. Led another expedition to Mount Makalu in 1960.

Houston, Dr. Charles S. (born 1913). American mountaineer. Joint-leader of the Anglo-American expedition which conquered Nanda Devi in 1936. Headed reconnaissance parties to Godwin Austen in 1938 and to Everest in 1950. Leader of the 1953 American expedition to Godwin Austen on which seven of the team members almost lost their lives in a heroic attempt to bring down a gravely-ill climber, Arthur Gilkey.

Hunt, Lord (born 1910). British mountaineer. Climbed extensively in the Alps in the 1930's and, in 1935 and 1936, made several ascents in the Karakoram range. Headed the British Everest expedition of 1953. His leadership and organization of this expedition were crucial

LAMBERT

LONGSTAFF

MALLORY

MERKL

factors in its ultimate success. In 1962, was joint-leader of an Anglo-Russian expedition to the Pamirs.

Lambert, Raymond (born 1914). Swiss mountaineer. Was one of a small party which made the second ascent of the north face of the Grandes Jorasses in 1935. Took part in the two Swiss expeditions to Everest in 1952. On the first of these, set a new height record by reaching 27,500 feet with Tenzing Norgay. Headed an expedition to Mount Gaurisankar, near Everest, in 1953.

Longstaff, Dr. Tom (1875–1964). British mountaineer and explorer. In 1905, became the first to reach and explore the Nanda Devi Ring. Explored Kamet with Charles Bruce in 1907, and, the same year, conquered Trisul, climbing the last 6,000 feet in one day, and setting a height record that remained unbroken for 20 years. In 1909, crossed the Saltoro Pass and explored the Siachen Glacier. Took part in the 1922 British Everest expedition. During his career, climbed in the Alps, the Caucasus, the Rockies, and Greenland.

Mallory, George Leigh (1886–1924). British mountaineer. Climbed extensively in the Alps in the early 1900's. Took part in the 1921 British reconnaissance of Everest and played a major part in exploring the North Col route. Became increasingly obsessed with conquering Everest, and took part in both the 1922 and the 1924 expeditions. On the second of these expeditions he lost his life, with Andrew Irvine, close to the summit of Everest.

Merkl, Willy (1900–1934). German mountaineer. Climbed in the Caucasus in 1929, and led the first German expedition to Nanga Parbat in 1932. Headed a second German assault on Nanga Parbat in 1934, and, on this attempt, died with several of his teammates high on the mountain during a blizzard.

Moore, Adolphus Warburton (1841–1887). British mountaineer. Climbed regularly in the Alps from 1860 to 1881. Was the first to climb Mont Blanc by the Brenva Ridge, in 1865. Made a lengthy tour through the Dauphiné Alps with Edward Whymper in 1864,

MOORE (RIGHT)

MUMMERY

ODELL

PACCARD

NOEL

NORTON

and took part in the first ascent of Les Ecrins. Accompanied Douglas Freshfield to the Caucasus in 1868 and, with him, made the first ascents of Kazbek and the east summit of Elbrus.

Mummery, Albert Frederick (1856–1895). British mountaineer. A leading exponent of the "new route" school of alpinism and a pioneer of guideless climbing. Made the first ascent of the Matterhorn by the Zmutt Ridge in 1879, and the first ascent of the Grépon in 1881. In 1888, visited the Caucasus and made the first ascent of Dykhtau. Between 1892 and 1894, made the first guideless ascents of the Grépon, the Brenva Ridge of Mont Blanc, and the Dent du Requin. Died during an attempted ascent of Nanga Parbat in 1895.

Noel, John (born 1890). British mountaineer. Climbed and explored in the Himalaya in 1913 and, on one occasion, succeeded in making his way to within 40 miles of Everest, closer than any European had ever come before. Took part, both as climber and photographer, in the British Everest expeditions of 1921, 1922, and 1924.

Norton, Edward F. (1884–1954). British mountaineer. Took part in the British Everest expedition of 1922. Led the 1924 Everest expedition on which he himself, climbing without oxygen, reached a height of 28,100 feet—higher than any man had yet climbed.

Noyce, Wilfrid (1919–1962). British mountaineer. Climbed extensively in the Alps and in Britain in the 1930's. Took part in the victorious British Everest expedition of 1953. Was killed in a fall during the ascent of Garmo Peak in the Pamirs in 1962.

Odell, Noel E. (born 1890). British mountaineer. Took part in the British Everest expeditions of 1922, 1924 and 1938. On the 1924 expedition, was the last man to see Mallory and Irvine alive, and the first to go in search of them. With Harold Tilman made the first ascent of Nanda Devi in 1936.

Paccard, Dr. Michel Gabriel (1757–1827). French doctor from Chamonix who, after several attempts, succeeded, with Jacques Balmat, in making the first historic ascent of Mont Blanc in 1786.

NOYCE (LEFT)

181

PECK

DE SAUSSURE

SELLA

Peck, Annie S. (1850–1935). American mountaineer. Began climbing in the Alps at the age of 45. In the course of a reconnaissance expedition to the Andes, climbed Mount Illampu (Sorata) in Bolivia. In 1908, climbed the north peak of Huascarán in Peru.

Saussure, Horace Bénédict de (1740–1799). Swiss naturalist and mountaineer. His firm belief that Mont Blanc could be climbed ultimately led to its first ascent by Paccard and Balmat in 1786. De Saussure himself climbed the mountain in 1787 and soon after spent two weeks on the Col du Géant carrying out scientific experiments. His life-long study of glaciers and mountain conditions laid the groundwork for later Alpine research.

Sella, Vittorio (1859–1943). Italian mountaineer-photographer. Climbed extensively in the Alps and the Caucasus in the 1880's and 1890's. Accompanied Abruzzi to Mount Saint Elias in 1897 and Freshfield to the Himalaya in 1899. Took part in Abruzzi's

SMYTHE

STEPHEN

SHIPTON (LEFT)

expeditions to the Ruwenzori range in 1906 and to the Karakoram range in 1909. His pictures taken on these expeditions are among the most beautiful mountain photographs ever produced.

Shipton, Eric Earle (born 1907). British mountaineer. Before 1931, took five expeditions to the mountains of eastern and central Africa. On one of these expeditions (in 1930) made the first ascent of Mount Kenya's Midget Peak with Harold Tilman. Was among the four men who reached Kamet on the British expedition of 1931. Took part in the British Everest expeditions of 1933, 1935 (which he led), 1936, and 1938. With Tilman in 1934, carried out a thorough reconnaissance of Nanda Devi and worked out routes to its summit. Led the 1951 British reconnaissance expedition to Everest which explored the southern approach route. In 1952, led an assault on Cho Oyu.

Smythe, Francis S. (Frank) (1900–1949). British mountaineer. Took part in expedition to Kanchenjunga in 1930. Led expedition that conquered Kamet in 1931, and was one of the four men to reach its summit. Took part in the British Everest expeditions of 1933, 1936, and 1938. During the course of his climbing career, made several new route ascents in the Alps and in the Canadian Rockies.

Stephen, Sir Leslie (1832–1904). British mountaineer and writer, whose book, *The Playground of Europe,* is still regarded as a classic statement of the mountaineer's attitude. Made numerous first ascents in the course of his long climbing career. Among these were the first climbs of the Zinal Rothhorn, the Schreckhorn, the Bietschorn, and Mont Mallet.

Streather, Tony (born 1926). British mountaineer. Took part in the Norwegian conquest of Tirich Mir in 1950, and was one of the three men to reach its summit. Was a member of the American expedition to Godwin Austen in 1953 and took part in the attempted rescue of Arthur Gilkey. Was one of the four men who reached the summit of Kanchenjunga on the British expedition of 1955. Led an attack on Haramosh, near Godwin Austen, in 1957.

Tenzing Norgay (born 1914). Sherpa of Darjeeling who, over the course of two decades, took part in no less than seven assaults on Everest. He joined his first Everest expedition as a porter in 1935. He soon became a climber in his own right, making the ascent of Kedarnath with the Swiss in 1947, and of Nanda Devi with the French in 1951. In 1952, he and the Swiss climber Raymond Lambert made two assaults on Everest (reaching, on the first attempt, a height of over 28,000 feet). In 1953, with Edmund Hillary, became the first to make the complete ascent of the world's highest peak.

Tilman, Harold William (born 1898). British mountaineer. As well as making the first ascent of Mount Kenya's Midget Peak in 1930, climbed Kilimanjaro and in the Ruwenzori range. With Eric Shipton carried out a thorough reconnaissance of the Nanda Devi Ring in 1934, and in 1936, led the expedition on which he and Noel Odell reached its summit. Took part in the British Everest expedition of 1935 and led the assault on Everest in 1938. In 1947, led a reconnaissance expedition which explored Rakaposhi and Mustagh Ata.

STREATHER

TENZING

TILMAN

TYNDALL

WASHBURN

In 1950, with Charles Houston, carried out a reconnaissance of Lhotse and the approach to Everest.

Tyndall, John (1820–1893). British mountaineer and scientist. Began visiting the Alps in 1856 for purposes of scientific research. By 1859, had climbed Mont Blanc three times. In 1861, made the first ascent of the Weisshorn.

Washburn, Bradford (born 1910). American mountaineer and explorer. Carried out extensive reconnaissance of the Alaskan ranges. Among his first ascents were Mount Lucania, Mount Sanford, Mount Marcus Baker, and Mount Saint Agnes in 1938. Climbed Mount McKinley in 1947 and 1951.

Whillans, Don (born 1933). British mountaineer. Has climbed extensively in the Alps and taken part in several Himalayan expeditions since 1957. In 1970, was a member of the British expedition to Annapurna, and, with Dougal Haston, was the first to reach its summit by the sheer south face route.

Wills, Sir Alfred (1828–1912). British mountaineer. Climbed extensively in the Alps during the 1850's. The most notable of his ascents was that of the Wetterhorn in 1854. This ascent, as he described it in *Wanderings Among the High Alps,* greatly stimulated British interest in alpinism, and is traditionally considered to be the climb that began the Golden Age of mountaineering.

Whymper, Edward (1840–1911). British mountaineer and artist. First visited the Alps in 1860 to make sketches for the Alpine Club. Made seven attempts on the Matterhorn before he conquered it in 1865, on the famous climb that ended in death for four of his party. Before the Matterhorn conquest, had made a number of first ascents, including that of Les Ecrins, Mont Dolent, the Aiguille Verte, and the west peak of the Grandes Jorasses. Later in his career climbed in Greenland (1879); in the Andes with his one-time rival Jean-Antoine Carrel (1880); and in the Canadian Rockies (1901, 1904, 1909) Wrote and illustrated a number of books, most notably *Scrambles Amongst the Alps in the Years 1860–69.*

Workman, Dr. William Hunter (1847–1932). American explorer and mountaineer who, with his wife Fanny Bullock Workman (1859–1925) made six exploratory expeditions to the Himalaya between 1899 and 1912. Their most important contribution, in 1912, was a reconnaissance and partial survey of the Siachen Glacier.

WHILLANS   WILLS (BELOW)

WHYMPER   WORKMAN

The Mountains

Right: this table provides pertinent information about some of the world's highest and most famous mountains. In cases where a mountain possesses more than one major peak, the date given for its first ascent is the year when its *highest* peak was first climbed. Every effort has been made, both here and throughout the text, to use the most up-to-date figures for mountain heights. However, the standard figure for the height of any mountain is liable to change slightly from year to year as the result of continually more accurate surveying techniques.

Mountain	Height	Location	First Ascent
HIMALAYA			
Mount Everest	29,028	Tibet/Nepal	1953
Mount Godwin Austen (K2)	28,250	Kashmir/China	1954
Kanchenjunga	28,168	Nepal/Sikkim	1955
Lhotse I	27,890	Tibet/Nepal	1956
Makalu I	27,824	Tibet/Nepal	1955
Cho Oyu	26,867	Tibet/Nepal	1954
Dhaulagiri	26,810	Nepal	1960
Nanga Parbat	26,660	Kashmir	1953
Manaslu	26,658	Nepal	1956
Nanda Devi	25,645	India	1936
Annapurna	26,504	Nepal	1950
Kamet	25,447	India	1931
Minya Konka	24,900	China	1932
Trisul	23,360	India	1907
PAMIRS			
Communism Peak	24,590	U.S.S.R.	1934
Lenin Peak	23,382	U.S.S.R.	1928
ANDES			
Aconcagua	22,834	Argentina	1897
Tupungato	22,310	Argentina/Chile	1897
Huascarán	22,205	Peru	1908
Yerupajá	21,758	Peru	1950
Coropuna	21,700	Peru	1911
NORTH AMERICA			
Mount McKinley	20,230	Alaska	1913
Mount Logan	19,850	Yukon	1925
Orizaba	18,701	Mexico	1848
Mount Saint Elias	18,008	Yukon/Alaska	1897
Popocatépetl	17,887	Mexico	1521
Mount Foraker	17,395	Alaska	1934
Mount Lucania	17,150	Yukon	1937
Mount Whitney	14,495	California	1873
AFRICA			
Kilimanjaro	19,340	Tanzania	1889
Mount Kenya	17,058	Kenya	1899
Margherita Peak	16,763	Uganda/Congo	1906
CAUCASUS			
Elbrus	18,481	U.S.S.R.	1868
Dykhtau	17,050	U.S.S.R.	1888
Koshtantau	16,875	U.S.S.R.	1887
ALPS			
Mont Blanc	15,781	France/Italy/Switzerland	1786
Monte Rosa	15,200	Switzerland/Italy	1855
Weisshorn	14,803	Switzerland	1861
Matterhorn	14,685	Switzerland/Italy	1865
Finsteraarhorn	14,026	Switzerland	1829
Grandes Jorasses	13,806	Switzerland	1868
Jungfrau	13,668	Switzerland	1811
Eiger	13,040	Switzerland	1858
Mittelhorn	12,166	Switzerland	1845
Wetterhorn	12,149	Switzerland	1854
Rosenhorn	12,110	Switzerland	1844

Below: this schematic diagram shows the comparative heights of the loftiest mountains in seven of the world's major mountain ranges.

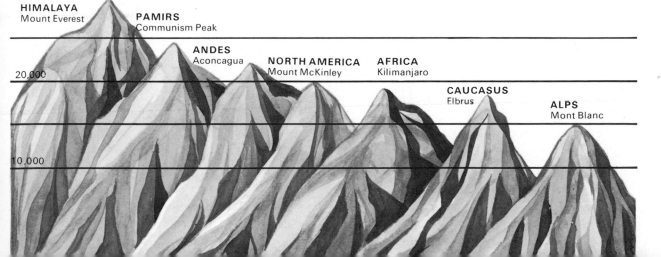

30,000

HIMALAYA
Mount Everest

PAMIRS
Communism Peak

ANDES
Aconcagua

NORTH AMERICA
Mount McKinley

AFRICA
Kilimanjaro

20,000

CAUCASUS
Elbrus

ALPS
Mont Blanc

10,000

Glossary

(For words not commonly used in English, the foreign derivation is given.)

acclimatization: In general, the process by which any organism accustoms itself to living in changed climatic conditions. In mountaineering, the process by which a man's body adjusts itself to functioning in the rarified atmosphere of higher altitudes.

aiguille: (French) a sharply pointed rock spire or peak.

alpenstock: (German) a long wooden staff with an iron point at one end used as a climbing aid until the second half of the 1800's, when it was replaced by the ice-ax.

alpinism: Mountain climbing in general, Alpine climbing in particular.

alpinist: A skilled mountaineer, especially one with considerable climbing experience in the Alps.

anorak: (Eskimo) a hooded jacket with tightly fitting cuffs and hip band designed for protection against wind, wet, and cold.

arête: (French) a particularly knife-like ridge or portion of a ridge.

artificial climbing: Climbing with the aid of a battery of specialized equipment, such as pitons, étriers, expansion bolts, and karabiners. Sometimes called "extreme climbing."

avalanche: A mass of snow, ice, and rock debris (sometimes weighing thousands of tons) which, when loosened by thaw or storm, becomes dislodged and hurtles down the face of a mountain, picking up more snow, ice, and rock as it falls.

barometer: An instrument used for measuring atmospheric pressure.

belay: To secure a rope by hitching it around a projecting rock, piton, or ice-ax, or by passing it around the body to ensure the safety of the man below. Also, the person or object which thus becomes an anchor.

bivouac: (French) to set up a temporary camp or improvised shelter. Also, the camp or shelter itself.

chamois: (French) a kind of goat-like antelope which inhabits the high passes of Europe and western Asia. It was once common in the Swiss Alps. Hunted for its extremely soft and pliable skin, from which "chammy" rubbing and polishing cloths are made.

chimney: A narrow, nearly-vertical cleft in a wall of ice or rock, just wide enough for a man to manoever in.

chronometer: A highly accurate timepiece used in the taking of measurements. Especially useful at high altitudes because it is unaffected by extremes of temperature or by changes in atmospheric pressure.

col: (French) a pass or depression in a mountain ridge, usually the lowest point between two peaks.

cornice: A mass of snow projecting outward from the top of a ridge like the crest of a wave.

couloir: (French) a wide gully on the side of a mountain, usually filled with ice and snow.

crampons: (French) frames with metal spikes strapped to the undersides of a climbers boots to give him a surer footing on ice and snow.

crevasse: (French) a deep crack or fissure in the surface of a glacier caused by stresses inside the mass of ice as it moves forward. Ranging from a few inches to many feet across, crevasses constitute one of the worst hazards of climbing. Some are masked by a treacherous covering of snow; others are spanned by slender ice bridges which may give way under the slightest pressure.

cwm: (Welsh) a narrow mountain valley or "armchair hollow" formed by glacial action.

direttissima: (Italian) the most direct route up a mountain face.

étrier: (French) a short rope ladder with several steps used as an aid in scaling sheer rockfaces. Originally the steps were made of wood, but today they are usually made of aluminum. The simplest form of étrier is a stirrup made of nylon webbing. Hung from a snap-link attached to a driven piton, the étrier affords a foothold where there is no natural crevice in the rock.

expansion bolt: A hollow metal sleeve which is hammered into rock that offers no cracks for a piton. Once the hollow bolt is driven in, a piton, slightly larger in diameter, can be inserted. Because the inside of the bolt is made of soft metal, it expands just enough to take the peg and hold it securely.

frostbite: The condition which results when, after prolonged exposure to extreme cold, the flow of blood to the extremities is cut off and the tissues become frozen. In mild cases, circulation can be restored by the gradual application of warmth, starting with snow or cold water, and by rubbing or slapping the affected areas. In more severe cases, injections of novaine acetychlorodine can be used to stimulate the flow of blood. But when frostbite is well advanced, it is impossible to restore the circulation, and the affected areas (usually fingers and toes) must be amputated, lest gangrene set in.

glacier: A river of packed ice (sometimes as much as 1,000 feet thick) which begins as an accumulation of snow in the upper slopes and hollows of a mountain. The weight of the snow causes this increasingly dense mass to move slowly down the mountain (at a rate which varies from a few inches to several feet a day) to the valleys below, where it melts and becomes a river. The movement of the glacier over steep or uneven terrain causes internal stresses which in turn produce cracks (crevasses) and contortions (icefalls and séracs) on its surface.

Gurkha: A native of Nepal belonging to a group of people who are Hindu in religion and almost always soldiers by profession.

hygrometer: An instrument for measuring the amount of moisture in the air.

hypsometer: An instrument for determining height above sea level by finding the boiling point of water. The boiling point, which depends on atmospheric pressure, is about 1°F. lower with each increase of 550 feet in altitude.

ice-ax: An essential tool for all snow and ice climbing. About three feet long, it is made of wood, with a metal spike at one end and a pickax at the other. Using the pickax, the climber can cut steps in the ice. By driving the pointed end deep into snow or ice, and passing his safety rope around the shaft, he can establish a belay, or anchor.

icefall: A particularly rough section of a glacier, having numerous crevasses, ice walls, and séracs.

karabiner: (German) a metal link that snaps shut. Used for joining two ropes or for hanging an étrier from the hole in a driven piton.

massif: (French) a compact portion of a mountain range with one or more summits, originating as a single block of the earth's crust.

meridian: A curved line drawn on the earth's surface from the north to the south pole. An arc of the meridian is any continuous portion of this line.

moraine: (French) a mass of boulders, rocks and gravel picked up by a glacier as it moves forward, and carried along on its surface.

melt-water: The water which streams down the face of a cliff when the snow and ice above begin to melt.

monsoon: The seasonal wind which blows northeast from the Indian Ocean in summer and southeast from Asia in winter. In India, the term is primarily used to mean the heavy rains which accompany the wind from June to September. With the onset of the monsoon, all Himalayan climbing must cease because of the increased risk of storms and avalanches.

mountain sickness: A disease which may afflict a climber at any height over 7,000 feet. Caused by an inadequate supply of oxygen to the blood and body tissues, mountain sickness manifests itself in a number of ways: headache, dizzyness, shortness of breath, rapid pulse, depression, and loss of concentration. Staged acclimatization can stave off these symptoms up to fairly extreme heights.

overhang: A massive bulge of rock on the face of a cliff.

oxygen apparatus: Equipment designed to feed oxygen-enriched air to the climber at extreme heights. First used on the British Everest expedition of 1922, oxygen apparatus has become increasingly sophisticated, and has played an important role in a number of Himalayan climbs in the past two decades. The use of oxygen not only increases the climber's strength and speed at high altitudes, but also ensures that his judgment and concentration will be unimpaired. The type of equipment most used today is called "open-circuit" and consists of a back-pack of oxygen cylinders, a flow-regulating device, a delivery tube, a storage bladder which keeps the oxygen ready for use and a face mask in which air and oxygen are mixed as the climber inhales.

piton: (French) a metal spike with a hole in one end, used in scaling sheer faces of rock or ice. Once a piton is driven into a crack in the surface, it can serve as a foothold, or an anchor from which to hang étriers or fixed ropes.

polariscope: An instrument for measuring or examining polarized light.

pundit: (Hindi) a wise or learned man. Indian surveyors employed by the British Survey Corps were called "pundit-explorers" because they were highly trained technicians as well as venturers into unknown territory.

ridge: A long narrow elevation of rock, sometimes covered with layers of snow and ice. The term can be used to describe either a steeply-rising crest leading to a summit, or a continuous chain of mountains.

sahib: (Hindi) a term of respect meaning "sir" or "master," used by Sherpa porters when addressing or speaking of the European mountaineers on a Himalayan expedition.

scree: A section of loose stones or rock debris on a mountainside.

sérac: (French) a wall or pinnacle of ice on the surface of a glacier. Subject to collapse at any time.

Sherpa: A member of a hill people who originally lived in Tibet and now inhabit the highlands of Nepal. Primarily farmers and mountain tradesmen, Sherpas possess remarkable strength and endurance. In the past four decades, Sherpas have served as porters on many Himalayan expeditions, and have distinguished themselves time and time again for their great courage and loyalty. Some, like Tenzing Norgay, have become expert mountaineers in their own right.

shoulder: A step-like leveling off of the contour of a ridge.

sirdar: (Hindi) the chief porter on a Himalayan expedition. The sirdar is the "head man" and it is his job to organize and assign tasks to the other Sherpas.

sky-hook: A metal claw with a rope attached which can be hooked into protrusions in a rockface and used as a belay, or anchor.

snow-blindness: A temporary, but extremely painful, loss or dimming of sight caused by the reflected glare of the sun on snow or ice. Can be prevented by wearing snow goggles or sunglasses in the heights.

sourdough: A nickname given to the prospectors and pioneers in the Yukon because of the sourdough bread that formed a staple part of their diet.

spur: The foot or lower part of a mountain ridge.

theodolite: A precision instrument with a telescopic sight used for determining angles.

traverse: To make a diagonal or horizontal crossing of a mountainside, or to travel from one side of a peak or pass to another. The term is also used to mean the technique involved in making such a crossing.

triangulation: A surveying technique in which the distance between two points or the relative position of two points is determined by dividing a geographical area into triangles and then measuring the bases and the angles formed by the triangles.

verglas: (French) the thin coating of ice which forms on a rock surface as rain and melt-water freeze on it.

Index

Picture Credits

Listed below are the sources of all the illustrations in this book. To identify the source of a particular illustration, first find the relevant page on the diagram opposite. The number in black in the appropriate position on that page refers to the credit as listed below.

1 Courtesy Alaska Historical Society Library
2 Aldus Archives
3 Alex Photography
4 The Alpine Club, London
5 The Alpine Club, London/Photo John Webb © Aldus Books
6 The American K2 Expedition, 1953
7 Archiv Deutsche Himalaja Stiftung, München/courtesy Paul Bauer
8 Bavaria Verlag, München
9 Martin Conway, *Climbing in the Karakorann Himalayas,* Ernest Benn Ltd., London
10 Bibliothèque Publique et Universitaire, Geneva
11 Courtesy Monsieur Pierre Bourrit/Photo Borel-Boissonnas
12 Musée d'Art et d'Histoire, Geneva (Collection La Fondation Gottfried Keller)/Photo Borel Boissonnas
13 Reproduced by permission of the Trustees of the British Museum
14 British Museum (Natural History)/Photo Michael Holford © Aldus Books
15 Brown Brothers
16 Camera Press
17 J. Allan Cash
18 Photo Riccardo Cassin
19 Photo John Cleare
20 Daily Telegraph Colour Library
21 Photo Glen Denny
22 Deutsches Institut fur Auslands-forschung, München
23 Photo C. M. Dixon
24 Photo Norman Dyhrenfurth
25 Mary Evans Picture Library
26 Fédération Française de la Montagne, Paris
27 Photo George Fisher
28 Photo Harrison Forman
29 Museum zu Allerhelligen, Schaffhausen/courtesy Orell Füssli Verlag, Zürich
30 Universitatsbibliothek, Erlangen/courtesy Orell Füssli Verlag, Zürich
31 Geographical Projects Limited, London
32 Gernsheim Collection, Humanities Research Center, The University of Texas at Austin
33 Dr. Georg Gerster
34 Photo Alfred Gregory
35 Photo T. Hiebelen
36 Belmore Browne, *The Conquest of Mt. McKinley*, Houghton Mifflin Company, Boston, Mass.
37 Photo Charles S. Houston
38 Photo I.T.N.
39 Reproduced by courtesy of India Office Library and Records, London
40 Reproduced by courtesy of India Office Library and Records, London/Photo R. B. Fleming © Aldus Books
41 Istituto Photographia Alpina V. Sella, San Gerolamo
42 Photo by Peter Larsen, A.R.P.S., F.R.G.S.
43 Magdalen College, Oxford
44 Mansell Collection
45 Courtesy Arnoldo Mondadori Ltd.
46 The Mount Everest Foundation
47 The Mount Everest Foundation (Annapurna South Face Expedition, 1970)
48 Courtesy Mountain Magazines Limited
49 Photo Josef Muench
50 Musée d'Histoire des Sciences, Geneva
51 National Portrait Gallery, London
52 Courtesy Captain John Noel
53 By courtesy of Captain Peter Norton
54 Novosti
55 Österreichische Galerie, Vienna/Photo Erwin Meyer
56 *Paris Match*/Photo Ichac
57 Photoworld
58 Picturepoint, London
59 Popperfoto
60 Galleria Borghese, Rome/Photo Mauro Pucciarelli
61 Museo Navale, La Spezia/Photo Mauro Pucciarelli
62 Palazzo dei Conservatori/Photo Mauro Pucciarelli
63 Radio Times Hulton Picture Library
64 Ronan Picture Library
65 Royal Geographical Society
66 Royal Geographical Society/Photo John Webb © Aldus Books
67 Royal Society, Edinburgh
68 Anton Schroll & Co., Wien
69 Photo Emil Schulthess
70 Schweizerische PTT Museum, Bern
71 Swiss Foundation for Alpine Research, Zürich
72 Swiss National Tourist Office, London
73 A. Tamari, Editore, Bologna
74 Three Lions, Inc.
75 Ullstein GMBH/Bilderdienst
76 Universitätsbibliothek, Erlangen-Nürnberg
77 Victoria & Albert Museum, London/Photo John Webb © Aldus Books
78 Bradford Washburn
79 Ian Yeomans/Susan Griggs Agency
80 Zentrale Farbbild Agentur, Düsseldorf

13		47			31	80	20	33	77	62	60	29 30	12	64	14
TITLEPAGE 4	5	4	5	6	7	8	9	10	11	12	13	14	15	16	17
	70	2		50 8	50	5 5	11	5	31	2	10		55	77	32 5
18	19	20	21	22	23	24	25	26	27	28	29	30	31	32	33
53 / 53		4	51 / 2	27 5 43 / 5		5 / 2	80	2 79 / 2		79	79	79 79 / 79		70	70
34	35	36	37	38	39	40	41	42	43	44	45	46	47	48	49
4	1	20	4	27 2	3	76 19 19 / 76		72 20 / 19		45	3	2 0 / 20	19	54	66
50	51	52	53	54	55	56	57	58	59	60	61	62	63	64	65
5 4 / 5	54	8 / 8	31	73	41 / 41	45	69	44 33		4	3	74 15	1	78 / 78	36 15
66	67	68	69	70	71	72	73	74	75	76	77	78	79	80	81
15 18 18 / 18		17	65	31	78	49 2	1	80	42	20 / 20	66	63		2 0 / 20	65
82	83	84	85	86	87	88	89	90	91	92	93	94	95	96	97
66 66 / 80		31	57		8	16	16	42		40	40	66	65 / 2	40 / 39	40
98	99	100	101	102	103	104	105	106	107	108	109	110	111	112	113
66	40 / 9		65 / 66	31		66 / 61	66	52		52	52	66	45	52 52	52
114	115	116	117	118	119	120	121	122	123	124	125	126	127	128	129
5	52 7	39 / 52		5	7	75	75	58	56		26	34	34	71 / 46	34
130	131	132	133	134	135	136	137	138	139	140	141	142	143	144	145
46	34	46	22 / 28	37	37 / 6	6 / 6	46 46	34	24		47	47		47	2
146	147	148	149	150	151	152	153	154	155	156	157	158	159	160	161
65 / 2	2	4 / 4	44	2 / 72	2	4 / 2	2	3 8 / 2	35	34 34 / 46	
162	163	164	165	166	167	168	169	170	171	172	173
41 73 / 4 45 / 4 7 2 19 19 52		75 / 68 / 18 / 19 44 43 72 46	65 / 78	41 65 67 19 22 16 / 65 34 / 19 6 / 46		71 65 52 2 52 4 / 75 52 / 52 / 2 46		15 25 / 65 / 59 46 63	6 / 71 / 46	51 / 78 / 48 / 53 72 2	
174	175	176	177	178	179	180	181	182	183	184	185